The Literature of Cinema

ADVISORY EDITOR: **MARTIN S. DWORKIN**
INSTITUTE OF PHILOSOPHY AND POLITICS OF EDUCATION
TEACHER'S COLLEGE, COLUMBIA UNIVERSITY

THE LITERATURE OF CINEMA presents a comprehensive selection from the multitude of writings about cinema, rediscovering materials on its origins, history, theoretical principles and techniques, aesthetics, economics, and effects on societies and individuals. Included are works of inherent, lasting merit and others of primarily historical significance. These provide essential resources for serious study and critical enjoyment of the "magic shadows" that became one of the decisive cultural forces of modern times.

The House That Shadows Built

William Henry Irwin

ARNO PRESS & THE NEW YORK TIMES

New York • 1970

Reprint Edition 1970 by Arno Press Inc.
Reprinted by Permission of Doubleday & Co., Inc.
Reprinted from a copy in The Museum of Modern Art Library
Library of Congress Catalog Card Number: 75-124012
ISBN 0-405-01618-2
ISBN for complete set: 0-405-01600-X
Manufactured in the United States of America

THE HOUSE THAT SHADOWS BUILT

Adolph Zukor

THE HOUSE
THAT SHADOWS BUILT

BY

WILL IRWIN

1928

DOUBLEDAY, DORAN & COMPANY, INC.

GARDEN CITY, NEW YORK

CONTENTS

BOOK I: BACKGROUNDS

BOOK II: STRUGGLE

BOOK III: FRUITION

LIST OF ILLUSTRATIONS

BOOK I
BACKGROUNDS

CHAPTER I

THE PENNY ARCADE

*T*HE Penny Arcade—it had no name more characteristic, and needed none—stood in 1904 near the point where East Fourteenth Street, crossing Broadway, forms the southern side of Union Square. I for one remember it well; there, a cub reporter fresh from the West, I used to indulge a passion for shooting with the miniature rifle. You paid twenty-five cents for a magazine of sixteen cartridges. That, in the Penny Arcade, seemed ostentatious spending. The standard unit of price for its other diversions and entertainments was one copper cent. By dropping such humble coin into a slot, you could make the automatic gypsy, who nodded reassuringly as she handed out the card, tell your fortune; you could obtain a horoscope with a portrait of your future husband or wife; you could stamp your name and address on an aluminum plate; you could hear, through two little insulators on a wire, the Floradora Sextette, Sousa's Band, or the ravings of John Mac-Coullough as transmitted by Edison's wonderful new invention the phonograph; you could punch the bag in competition with the records of Corbett, Jeffries, Fitzsimmons, and Terry McGovern; you could test your

3

resistance to the electric current or your lifting capacity. Finally, at the magic of the same little red coin, you could peer into a black eye-piece and witness such tabloid silent drama as *The Servant Girl's Dream* or *Fun in a Boarding School*. This, the first entity of the moving picture, was the most popular machine in the Penny Arcade. The dramas lasted as long as three quarters of a minute; and on Saturday nights a queue, with pennies in hand, waited its turn at the eye-piece.

The managers of this pioneer enterprise chose their location shrewdly. Union Square was once heart and centre of the Broadway theatrical district. However, a decade or so before the Penny Arcade arrived, the theatres had suddenly hopped a dozen blocks northward and settled about Madison Square. The wave of immigration from southern and eastern Europe was just then rising to its full tide. From the south and east, the immigrants pressed on Union Square, which presently became their playground and political rallying-point. The Academy of Music lay a block eastward on Fourteenth Street. Once its very name suggested wealth and social eminence; now it became a German theatre. Between its site and the square lay old mansions and business buildings which in their time had housed wealthy residents or dispensed the latest Parisian fashions. Saloons and dance halls took them over. Some of the dancing establishments were very tough; some merely cheap and joyful. Tom Sharkey, his ribs permanently damaged by his last fight with Jeffries, set up on this row his saloon and dance hall. He had been pride and champion of the United States Navy. Jack ashore thereupon abandoned the Bowery and rushed to Fourteenth Street. When the fleet lay in New York Harbour, the sidewalks seemed to rock with the rolling gait of bluejackets and marines.

Nightly, immigrant folk too timid and ill at ease to venture into the sophisticated white-light district crowded Union Square. The family groups among them cared little for the dance halls—they were too disreputable and expensive. The Penny Arcade, however, was a "first-class family resort," and cheap. For twenty-five cents you could enjoy twenty-five separate and distinct forms of entertainment. The strength-testing devices made an urgent appeal to the bluejackets; by whole starboard watches, they raided the punching bag, the weights, the hammer device. Anyone with half an eye for business must have seen that this novel enterprise was making money.

A year or so later, uptowners who wandered into Fourteenth Street noticed that the Penny Arcade seemed to have expanded. The building next door, until recently a saloon, was now furnished forth with a crude marquee over which glowed the sign "Comedy Theatre" and from which hung violent lithographs. These portrayed thief chases, train robberies, and similar thrilling violences; and a lettered strip, annexed to the lower border, announced that the Comedy showed moving pictures. For the cinema had of late emerged from the little boxes which still occupied the Penny Arcade next door and—much against the judgment of Thomas A. Edison, its chief inventor—had taken timidly to a toy screen. Basement establishments on the East Side were already exhibiting European films with stories, incidents, and costumes shocking to the morals of the period; we heard the first growls of censorship. But the Comedy Theatre, like the Penny Arcade next door, stuck to "high-class family entertainment." Though heroes shot villains and yeggs blew safes in full view of the audience and in defiance of our modern police regulations, no line or episode brought the blush to the most modest cheek. Presently, the Penny Arcade itself opened a "picture show"—admission five cents—on the floor above.

A few years of this; and Fourteenth Street underwent another transformation. A Tammany clean-up wiped out the dance halls; presently prohibition was to do away with the saloons. It became the cheapest of all cheap shopping streets. The Penny Arcade and the Comedy Theatre disappeared, along with the more disreputable sister-establishments lying to eastward. A miniature department store whose windows exhibit three-dollar-and-ninety-six-cent dresses and one-dollar-and-forty-three-cent hats now occupies the site. Only a few New Yorkers remember them—they were so humble, of so little consideration!

Yet that site at 46 and 48 Union Square South deserves, I think, its brass tablet. For here the gods of destiny made magic. Black muck in the bottom of a pond; and from that, by the incomprehensible legerdemain of nature, blows a water lily, the whitest thing in nature. Brown, common dirt in the bottom of a crucible; and from that oozes gold. The Penny Arcade was "over-owned." Into it had come several men of very humble origin; mostly immigrants who landed before the Federal Government required each newcomer to possess fifty dollars in cash—on the new terms, they could never have landed at all. When they finished with the Penny Arcade and branched out from it, they were on their way to wealth and power. All succeeded beyond any reasonable dream of an immigrant boy. Most, indeed, became millionaires; and two, Adolph Zukor and Marcus Loew by name, many, many times millionaires.

That, perhaps, is enough to justify this story of the Penny Arcade in South Union Square; what flowed into it and what emerged. However, there is a larger justification. The partners in this merry and amusing venture—and especially Zukor—were within a few years to take the moving picture out of our poorer quarters and set it into the heart of cities; were to serve destiny as chief agents in making it the third or fourth American industry, for financial importance and the activity by which the American mind, in the second and third decades of the Twentieth Century, stamped most deeply its imprint on the Old World.

It will be necessary now to go back to the beginnings of many things; to trace from their sources several currents of life which flowed in 1904 into the Penny Arcade, South Union Square. Let us begin with the leading character: Adolph Zukor of Ricse, Hungary.

CHAPTER II

THE ORPHAN OF RICSE

*T*HE town of Ricse lies on the borders of the Tokay wine district in Hungary. It has—and has had since the dawn of its recorded history—less than two thousand inhabitants. It does not differ in essentials from a myriad of other little farming centres scattered over the face of Europe. There is a main street of settled gray-stone buildings; a square with a town hall; a fringe of small houses with flagged and scrubbed front steps. Land is precious and the houses huddle so close together that one seems to be living in a community building with every other inhabitant. The farms, checkerboarded between low stone walls, come up to the very pavements. As generally throughout Europe, the farmers lodge in town and go forth to their cultivating on foot or on the backs of their work horses. Life is rooted in the soil. The banker deals in lands; and even the store-keepers till their little inherited patches of five or ten acres.

To this class of small tradesmen belonged the Zukors. As far back as exact family history ran, they had owned a succession of humble shops at Ricse. They had been Hungarians for so many generations that they, like the

9

rest of Ricse, stood rooted in the soil. In the 'sixties of the last century, just when the current of world politics was carrying Hungary into the arms of Austria and to a German overlordship which provincial Ricse loathed, Jacob Zukor, a younger son, owned and ran the little general store.

Now among the tradesmen of Ricse was a newcomer, Nathan Liebermann by name. He sprang from Sina, a small town up in the hills where they make the Tokay wine. The Liebermanns had a different background from the Zukors, though they, too, had lived time out of mind in Hungary. From grandfather to father to son, they passed on the rabbinical tradition. The oldest boy was devoted at his birth to service of the temple, and in some generations, all the boys. If they felt no call to religion the men of the Liebermanns usually became physicians. Always they had saved and scrimped from the tiny wages of country clergymen to give the boys a higher education. Nathan was an exception. He felt no call to the clergy, to medicine, to any intellectual occupation. Having acquired a little store in Sina, he sold it and moved to Ricse, which offered greater opportunity.

To him, shortly after his removal, came visiting his sister Hannah. Elderly Ricse still remembers her as a young girl of singularly delicate beauty. Jacob Zukor, visiting his competitor, beheld her and fell almost violently in love. So, for that matter, did Hannah Liebermann. The affair ran the normal course. They married, and Hannah Zukor exchanged the economical gentility of a country parsonage for a hard life as wife to a peasant storekeeper. They had three sons. The first died in early infancy. Five years later came Arthur, vigorous and bright from his birth; and two years after (January 7, 1873) a small but healthy and well-formed boy whom they named Adolph.

When Adolph was one year old and Arthur three, Jacob Zukor essayed one day to lift a heavy box. He strained himself, broke a vein. That seemed only a minor accident until blood poisoning set in; and after much suffering, he died. Left alone with two small children, Hannah Zukor did the only thing possible for a woman of her time and place. The business was her sole asset for bringing up her children. That a woman should conduct a shop seemed an impossible thought for the Ricse of the time when Emperor Franz Josef was young. With frank reluctance, she married again. From that day she went into a decline and when Adolph was seven years old, she died. Her surviving relatives do not even remember what the doctors named as her malady, so certain are they of the real cause—a broken heart. That marriage to Jacob Zukor had been a singularly close and personal union; "they were wrapped up in each other." When he died, her world went away from her.

If I mention this intimate detail, it is by way of proving an old-fashioned and sentimental theory. This marriage produced two extraordinary man-children. Both

Arthur and Adolph lived to create for themselves distinguished careers, though along strangely diverse lines. And our fathers held that the best children spring from harmony and perfect love. That, however, is one human value which eugenics cannot weigh in the scales of science.

What was going to happen to little Arthur and little Adolph? For a year, the Zukors and Liebermanns argued the question. Patently their stepfather did not want them; as a matter of fact, in a year or so he married again. By the law of the Dual Monarchy, the slender proceeds from sale of their father's property passed into possession of the state, which would deliver the interest, as needed, to their lawful guardians and would pay them the principal when they came of age. The interest might furnish them with clothes, medical attendance, school books, and trimmings. It would not suffice to pay their board. Adolph Zukor still remembers his eighth year as a period of dreadful and gloomy uncertainty. He knows now for what he waited. Rabbi Kalman Liebermann, his maternal uncle, was steeling himself to a great sacrifice.

A little after his sister's marriage, Kalman had taken over the synagogue at Szalka, a town ten miles away, to which little Ricse was as a metropolis. Arthur, his sister's oldest boy, was a brilliant child; and even the quieter Adolph showed promise. If someone would board them, give them guidance, the inheritance might provide for their higher education—often the official guardians granted to a promising orphan boy a part of his capital in advance of his twenty-first year. With care, economy, and sacrifice, it might be done. And his dead sister, true to her family tradition, had wished to dedicate these sons of hers to religion. Rabbi Kalman Liebermann decided to accept the burden; and in a country diligence, Adolph and Arthur journeyed to Szalka.

There followed six years of close living in a village parsonage, and of peaceful monotony. The orphans entered the common school at Szalka. Arthur had already a year or two of primary education; but it was a new experience for Adolph. Arthur was born with the gift of expression. He went ahead fast—the bright boy of every class in which he found himself. Also, he was beginning to show that spirituality which marked his mature career. He was always playing at preaching, with his schoolmates, his cousins, and Adolph as congregation.

As for Adolph—it was harder to tell. Somewhat under the shadow of this brilliant elder brother, he turned out a quiet boy with a placid front overlying a hot temper. He showed little or none of the family talent for expression. His favourite study was geography; but he got his best marks in arithmetic. In Hungarian language and literature he graded only fair; and in German, then a required study of all schools in the Dual Monarchy, he just crowded past the mark that designated failure. So life went placidly until at the age of thirteen Adolph was graduated from the grade school and stood ready to go on to the *Gymnase*, equivalent to our high school, whither the brilliant Arthur had preceded him two years before. Adolph was small for his age; a healthy, active, energetic boy, but silent and thoughtful.

One person seems to have perceived some unusual quality underlying Adolph's reserved exterior. Samuel Rosenberg, the head master, had won his shy confidence. As Adolph packed up his books for the last time, he came suddenly out of his shell and told this sympathetic teacher the thought of his heart. In the way he seemed destined to go, he saw no promise; for he was not especially religious and he lacked the essential gift for speaking. If he passed on to the *Gymnase* and to some higher school, life offered only one alternative: he could become a country notary, keeping up appearances on the income of a minor clerk. Medicine, that traditional second choice of the Liebermanns, was impossible in his case; the estate could not support the long years in college and professional school. He wanted to do something else —he didn't know exactly what, but something practical, something active.

This is the substance of the conversation as Adolph Zukor remembered it forty years later. One can only imagine its boyish exaggerations and despairs. The fact that neither he nor his teacher conceived of any career for an educated man except that of notary or village rabbi illustrates the narrow outlook of the circle into which he was born.

Samuel Rosenberg listened sympathetically, drew him out, and then did a thing which Adolph Zukor was long in forgiving. Impelled by sense of duty, he reported the conversation to Kalman Liebermann. The Rabbi took it hard. Although Adolph held up his end in the subsequent family row, he sympathized a little and sympathizes wholly now with his uncle's point of view. Rabbi Liebermann, in taking on these two orphans, had performed an act of pure sacrifice to the memory of a favourite sister and to religion. It had forced the Liebermanns to live so closely that every pinch of salt and every pin counted. "A new pair of shoes," said Adolph Zukor years later, "was an event." And in the case of Adolph, the sacrifice had gone in vain. When at last the Rabbi cooled off, he did the sensible thing.

As I have said already, Szalka is ten miles from Ricse. Ten miles in another direction lies Szanto, a small wine-growing centre. There Herman Blau, well and favourably known to Kalman Liebermann, kept the big general store. A few weeks later Adolph Zukor, taking his initial step into the outer world, travelled to Szanto by diligence with his articles of apprenticeship in his pocket. By their terms he must serve Herman Blau truly and faithfully for the space of three years.

Apprenticeship in Hungary does not differ essentially

from that gloomy servitude of the English draper's shop with which H. G. Wells has acquainted us in *Mr. Polly* and *The Wheels of Chance*. The apprentices sleep in a one-room dormitory over the shop, eat below the salt with the shopkeeper's family. When he deposited his bundle beside his cot, Adolph discovered four other apprentices, all peasant boys from the surrounding fields. The conversation and the pranks that night shocked him to his marrow. Plain living and high thinking stood the unexpressed motto of the Liebermann family. "Uncle Kalman," said Zukor in his maturity, "was marooned in the country, but he was a big man. He hadn't gone to seed, and he hadn't become a fossil." At that country parsonage, one heard constant discussion on things of the mind and of the spirit; especially, Kalman Liebermann had trained his brood in purity of thought and correctness of Hungarian speech. Adolph's citified ways and grammatical speech irritated the yokels; and his small stature tickled their crude sense of humour. "I felt," says Zukor, "as though someone had dropped me into a sewer." After the evening's hazing, he lay awake in the darkness, stuffing the bedclothes into his mouth and resisting the temptation to run away —back to the congenial home of Rabbi Liebermann. But pluck and pride, two of his governing qualities, pulled him through. And when next morning Herman Blau taught him how to wrap up bundles, his spirits began to mount,

Within six months, his industry and intelligence made him the favourite apprentice. The Blaus, and especially the large brood of Blau daughters, liked him; virtually took him into the family. Though comparatively un-educated, they were reading people; and they shared their books with him. It was not "serious reading," however. They liked adventure and romance, a kind of literature which Kalman Liebermann excluded from his own library as frivolous and dispiritualizing. Adolph devoured the standard Hungarian novelists, and, in translation, the great western European romancers like Dumas and DeFoe. Also, the American dime novel—translated, of course—enjoyed a vogue in Hungary. Just as in the land of its origin, careful parents forbade the dime novel to children. However, one of the younger Blau girls was secretly an addict; and she slipped worn copies on to Adolph. From their tales of Indians and cowboys, of poor boys suddenly grown rich, he found a romantic picture of America. Probably the American dime novel was the primary cause of his subsequent migration.

But for this taste of the Blaus he would have gone unbooked. His apprenticeship furnished his board and lodging. and nothing more. Twice a year, he drew upon the little estate of his father a requisition for his other necessities. His first experience taught him to ask for more than he needed. One suit of clothes, one hat, one pair of shoes, so many shirts, suits of underwear, socks

—and a few trimmings, thrown in not because Adolph really expected them but because they furnished a margin for pruning. The list went first to his uncle Ignatz Zukor at Ricse; for he, and not the philanthropic but impractical Kalman Liebermann, stood as official guardian to Arthur and Adolph. Ignatz Zukor inspected the list and cut it down according to his ideas of what was good for a growing boy. Then the banker who held the fund in trust took his turn and filed off the edges. Their system made no allowance for such frivolous luxuries as books or spending-money. Until he finished his apprenticeship at the age of fifteen, Adolph Zukor had never jingled in his pocket a single copper coin which he could call his own.

The term of indenture expired early in the summer of 1888. Adolph had grown by now so valuable to the store that Herman Blau, instead of sending him out with a blessing to find a job, asked him to stay on as assistant at a salary equivalent to two American dollars a month and board. But that, the first real money he had ever earned, brought no thrill of accomplishment to young Adolph Zukor. Instead, it seemed again to mark and to symbolize the narrowness of the goal toward which he had been making for the past three years. Just as when he left grammar school, he sat down and deliberated on his present and future. By renouncing a higher education, he had only reached another impasse, bound himself to another wheel. For some years, he would receive this meagre salary. Successive raises might bring it to eight dollars American a month; the very height of expectation in that direction. When he came of age, he would receive his share of the inheritance. With that, he could perhaps buy a minority partnership in Blau's store, or start a very humble shop of his own. Beyond— nothing.

His constant reading had given him a picture of the world outside; a little lurid, perhaps, but accurate in its main outlines. He had begun to see in perspective the triangle of farming country bounded by Ricse, Szanto, and Szalka. For a man of ambition, it was hopeless. People were born, grew up, mated, bred offspring, worked until death with no aim or object except providing for to-day's necessities. None dreamed of rising above his father's level in society. At the other pole stood glittering America, where men of ambition achieved miracles. For though he was growing old and wise enough not to swallow all the details of the translated dime novels, the glamour of their atmosphere lingered in his mind. Also, a few other young men of the Ricse district had felt the stirrings of adventure and sailed for New York. They wrote of wages as high as ten or fifteen dollars a week. To prove it, they were sending remittances to their parents.

He had no money for his passage—but there was the little inheritance. The Orphans' Bureau of the Austro-Hungarian government had the right to draw in necessity upon the principal. With Arthur's share they proposed soon to do exactly that. Arthur, having finished the *Gymnase* in a blaze of glory, was going on to the University at Berlin. For Kalman Liebermann saw in this brilliant elder nephew not only a real rabbi but a jewel of the Temple. Officially Kalman adopted him; he went on his career, which fulfilled all the early expectations, as Arthur Liebermann.

Before young Adolph had drawn the wages of his second month, his gloomy meditations crystallized into decision. He would go to America; and the estate must pay his passage. Immediately he set on foot a series of adolescent diplomacies. Herman Blau was the first obstacle. When Adolph, on closing his apprenticeship, accepted service in the general store, he had bound himself to stay with the job for a year. Through all his early, struggling career, impatience was his personal devil; the alloy of his splendid energies. That year seemed an eternity.

"I want to go to America," he said when he summoned the courage to have it out with his employer. "Right away—this autumn."

·On the American question, Herman Blau was open-minded. His own daughter had married and emigrated to New York; her husband had found a good job in a department store. He, too, believed that America made magic. On the other hand, he disliked to lose an assistant so cheap and valuable.

"Wait until your year is out," he said. Plainly, he believed that by then Adolph might get over the notion.

Whereupon Adolph fell into a melancholy decline; half genuine, half assumed. The Blau daughters, who regarded this quiet little apprentice boy as a brother and who had themselves a dime-novel picture of America, threw in their powerful influence on his side. At last, Herman Blau gave a reluctant consent. Adolph might go—and whenever he wished.

The next and harder obstacle was his uncle and guardian. Adolph knew Ignatz Zukor, farmer, shopkeeper, and miller, for a stiff-necked and conservative man. He would need special treatment. Adolph scribbled for days in composing a letter which would begin the process of melting him. In this little masterpiece, he not only recited his reasons for wanting to emigrate, but he exaggerated his miseries and introduced sinister, insincere hints at self-destruction. The first sentence of Ignatz Zukor's hasty answer had an emotional tone which indicated that the plot was working.

"My dear Nephew," it began. "You always seemed a sensible boy. Therefore I am astounded. . . ." However, there was no hurry. "Let us look into the matter. Let us write to Dr. Gustavus Liebermann." Gustavus was a cousin of Adolph's who had gone to New York and established a practice on Lexington Avenue. Nothing to do now but wait.

In a month, Ignatz Zukor sent the reply of Cousin Gustavus. America, it said, was a hard place for the new immigrant. Ignorant of the language, he always found difficulty in getting a job. Often he became a public charge; just as often he gave it up and wrote home for money. Gustavus would not wish a cousin of his to take such chances.

"You see. . . ." wrote Uncle Ignatz Zukor.

But America had become an obsession with Adolph. He renewed his importunities and his sinister hints.

"Well," wrote Uncle Ignatz at last, "come here and talk it over."

So Adolph bade a confident farewell to the Blaus, and walked to Ricse with his few belongings on his back. To-day, he is a rather silent man except when he has something significant to say; then he can become most eloquent and persuasive. Perhaps he had these same traits even in his adolescence. At any rate, in two or three days he had won over Uncle Ignatz.

Last and greatest obstacle was that town banker who, in matters concerning the little Zukor estate, acted as deputy for the Orphans' Bureau. Uncle Zukor made an appointment for a hearing on the matter. Adolph lay awake nights composing his selling-talk. He was still undersized; as he delivered it, his head scarcely appeared above the banker's high desk. This fervid oration was probably a charming mixture of tragic juvenile emotion and premature common sense. For the banker listened, and finally agreed. He was about to sign the paper which would send Adolph to America when his expression stiffened. He dropped his pen and called Ignatz Zukor aside.

"Suppose," he said, "that this boy has committed some crime or faces some disgrace and wants to emigrate in order to escape the consequences!"

"He has queer notions, but he was always a good boy," maintained Uncle Ignatz Zukor.

"I cannot accept that assurance from a relative," replied the banker. "I must delay my decision until I communicate with his employer."

Adolph waited three days more. Then came a postcard:

Adolph hat nicht verschuldet. [Adolph has done nothing wrong.]
HERMAN BLAU.

So with their apprehensive blessing, his relatives hipped little Adolph Zukor to America. Uncle Ignatz bought his ticket—third class—straight through to Berlin; his aunts and cousins packed in a straw hamper provision for the journey. At Berlin, Arthur Liebermann took him from the train and led him to his own little student room. They had not trusted Adolph with the steamer-ticket; Arthur had bought that and was holding it for him. Also, the estate had granted the equivalent of forty dollars for his start in the New World. Arthur changed this into American bills. With his own hand, he sewed these into the lining of Adolph's second-best waistcoat. Next, the trip to Hamburg—Arthur put his ticket personally into the hands of the conductor—and finally, the steamer *Russia*.

This was one of those decrepit little baskets which plied between Germany and the United States in the 'eighties; the great American merchant marine lingered in the womb of time. The steerage was incredibly foul, morally as well as physically. As yet, we were enforcing no restrictions whatever on immigration. The ship's company represented the scum of Europe, mixed with a little of the unrisen cream—like that undersized boy of sixteen now beginning to experience distressing symptoms in his upper berth. After one look at his surroundings, he had decided that it would be more hygienic not to undress. He wore his second-best suit, with the forty dollars sewed into the lining, through a seventeen-day voyage during which he never left his berth. To this day, Adolph Zukor looks forward to a sea voyage as to a major illness.

"Lucky I didn't undress," he said years later. "With the company I was keeping, the forty dollars wouldn't have lasted forty minutes! They were robbing each other all through the voyage."

There were no landing formalities. The *Russia* simply ran up to the sea wall at Castle Garden, lashed alongside, and drove its passengers ashore. Zukor, like Pupin and Schurz before him, stepped on to the soil of the New World at Battery Park, an unconsidered little animal in a filthy and bedraggled human herd.

It was early evening of an autumn day in 1888. The downtown business district had not yet closed up shop and gone home to dinner, but darkness had begun to fall; and all the windows glistened with that new metropolitan marvel, electric lights. In the foreground at Number One Broadway stood the pioneer twelve-story skyscraper, highest office building in the world; a tower of luminescence. Adolph Zukor carries to this day a memory of the exaltation which bathed his soul.

Let us look him over as he steps ashore. Not long afterward he had his photograph taken, and a print survives. It shows a comely, swarthy-skinned boy with bright, expressive eyes—hazel brown in the flesh—firm brows, a nose just slightly aquiline, a mouth which closed as tight as a trap, a round, compact head with a thatch of close-cropped, raven-black hair. This runs to a "widow's peak" in front and seems formed to match a pointed depression at the middle of his upper lip. He had not yet reached his full growth; and he was never to reach five feet four inches in stature. But it was a finely formed little body, both wiry and rugged. His small feet, even now, point straight forward like an Indian's; and he can walk forever.

Already, as this brief narrative proves, he had begun to show the courage with life, the judgment and the ambition which made his subsequent career. Whence first sprang the ambition—in the unaspiring atmosphere of Ricse—one would find it hard to say. Such traits, modern psychologists tell us, take hold of the soul in those years before the mind begins to make conscious records. The Liebermanns, his mother's family, had always shown more urge for eminence than the other people of their circle; and perhaps the broken-hearted Hannah Liebermann planted this seed in both her sons. Further, emulation of his brother Arthur, for whom Kalman Liebermann was doing so much, had its distinct influence on Adolph.

His education, so far, was of such sort as to fit him for that career which, after many vicissitudes, he would enter fifteen years later—the expansion of the moving picture into a major American industry. His schooling had not passed beyond what we call in America the eighth grade. However, European education was then much more thorough then American. And from his school or his innate qualities, he had acquired the best practical fruit of education—the orderly mind. He thinks on straight lines; he has a passion for seeing things as they are. In that respect, he is perhaps innately educated. Had he gone on like his brother Arthur to the University, he might have done great things; but probably not with the moving picture. That needs the common touch, which a higher education usually dulls. Even his reading had helped him along the road which he was to travel. He read by habit "for the story." If he were called upon to list the books that have helped him, he would have to include the American dime novel!

Then as now he had a deep-running nature, at bottom romantic and sentimental. But then as now he hid it under a face which, in emotional stress, became a mask. Essentially, he was as shy as an Englishman; and, like an Englishman, least expressive when most deeply moved.

CHAPTER III

CASTLE GARDEN

SEWED into the lining of his second-best waistcoat beside the precious forty dollars, Adolph treasured a notebook with the addresses of a few Ricse people who had transplanted themselves to New York. Dr. Gustavus Liebermann, his cousin, headed the list. However, the doctor had advised against his emigration. Adolph felt none too sure of his welcome in that quarter—especially since he looked, after his fortnight in an upper bunk, like a specimen from a garbage pail. Next in order was a certain Mrs. Lowy who, as an older girl, had played with the Liebermann children in Ricse.

On the edge of Battery Park stood drawn up a line of express wagons. An experienced Hungarian from the steerage told him that these conveyances made a business of transporting passengers and their goods. Adolph approached the nearest wagon and showed Mrs. Lowy's address. The driver nodded, helped him pile his luggage aboard, drove him to a tenement in Second Street, took a fifty-cent piece from the handful of change which Adolph proffered, and helped find Mrs. Lowy's door.

When that opened, Mrs. Lowy stared for a half minute at this little scarecrow and then fell on its neck.

Plying him with questions about Ricse and Ricse people, she prepared him the first meal he had been able to
retain for a fortnight. This finished, she got his best suit
out of his little hair-cloth trunk, pressed it, filled the
wash-tub with hot water, and left him alone in the kitchen for a scrub. His self-respect restored, Adolph felt
less timid about Cousin Gustavus. He slept that night in
a scratched-up bed on the floor of Mrs. Lowy's parlour;
and next morning enquired his way to the doctor's office
in Lexington Avenue.

Gustavus proved an agreeable disappointment. "Come
and stay with me until you find something to do," he
said. So Adolph transferred his hair-cloth trunk from
the tenement of the hospitable Mrs. Lowy to the doctor's uptown flat.

Nevertheless, Dr. Gustavus had in the pessimistic
letter told the truth. There seemed small chance of
Adolph getting a job until he learned something of the
difficult, unfamiliar English language. Six months at
school might turn the trick, but Adolph had no funds to
keep him going meanwhile. Dr. Gustavus put out
feelers in the Hungarian colony. They came to nothing.
An undersized, greenhorn boy without a trade or without English seemed a worthless piece of human material.

Meantime, Adolph walked the streets of Manhattan;
a gaping young rustic in a strangely cut suit of old-
country clothes. He had whirled through Budapest,
Vienna, and Berlin, seeing little beyond the railroad

station. Now, he had at the same time his first view of his new world and of a great city. There were as yet no skyscrapers except that twelve-story building at Number One Broadway; but all things human are relative, and the six-story office buildings seemed to pierce the clouds. The automobile was a decade away; but down Broadway ran end to end public conveyances with no engine before or behind—propelled as by force of circumstances. Overhead clattered the Elevated; itself just lately electrified.

He stood on Fifth Avenue, reviewing the afternoon parade of hansoms, of private carriages with footmen on the boxes and ladies lolling within. He dodged through the splendours of the Ladies' Mile on Broadway, watching the bustled and coiffured peacocks ply their shopping—such women as his adolescent imaginings had never dared dream on. He stood fascinated before the array of big diamonds in the window of Tiffany's, Union Square. He must have glanced diagonally across the square to a row of conservative four-story buildings housing on their ground floor "specialties for ladies." No flash of prescience told him that there, fifteen years later and when all the glory was gone from old Union Square, he would begin to build his fortune. . . . A year or so later, Thomas Alvah Edison sent to Oscar King Davis of the New York *Sun* a cryptic message about "something new." Davis rushed to the laboratory at East Orange. Edison made him apply his eye to a little chute covered with black cloth. Davis beheld a lighted piece of glass. Upon it appeared the photograph of a man. It glittered oddly. Then the man began to move. Jerkily, the image skipped, danced, leaped. . . .

At night, young Adolph Zukor wandered up the theatrical zone of Broadway where that new marvel, the electric light, illuminated the posters of Booth in classical tragedy, of Ada Rehan in classical comedy. Between the theatres, swinging doors opened into gilded and glittering saloons, from which floated the lively rattle of masculine talk and laughter. This brilliant quarter mile ended before Broadway widened out into Longacre Square; an irregular quadrangle of shops and bars housed in what had been fine old residences.

Again, prescience withheld its magic. No thrill foretold the Paramount Building, built on the increment of shadows, guarding the gateway to a new city of light. . . . The crowds, thronging the streets pavement-full, did not overawe and depress him as they do so many who behold the great metropolis for the first time. Weaker spirits, come to New York in search of fortune, have terminated their adventuring in the first three weeks, unable to endure the overwhelming impersonality of this river of souls. But they inspired him; he fell in love on sight with the metropolis.

The exalted interest of this mood alternated with anxiety. Dr. Gustavus could find him no job. When his quandary took hold of him, Adolph always walked over to the East Side and unbosomed himself to the warm and understanding Mrs. Lowy. She was working in her own way. On the third Sunday of the Zukor invasion of America, she called together the Hungarian denizens of her tenement house for a symposium on the burning question: what could be done about Adolph?

An upholsterer spoke up. "Maybe the boy can't stand the work," he said, "but they're looking for an apprentice in my shop."

Next morning, Adolph presented himself to the foreman and was engaged at two dollars a week. The foreman put him to tacking covers on sofas. You knelt on the spring upholstery, forced it down with your weight, pulled the cover into place, and drove home the tack. Naturally clever with his hands, Adolph Zukor caught the trick in a day. But his size proved a distressing handicap. He weighed less than a hundred pounds. Where the heavyweights working beside him forced down the springs without difficulty, he lived through a perpetual wrestling match. After two weeks of this, he felt his strength passing; plainly, he was not born for an upholsterer. Then, as he walked heavily home from work on the second Saturday night, a voice hailed him in Hungarian from a front stoop—Max Gross of all people! Max was one of those peasant apprentice boys at Blau's store who had given him that spiritual hazing on his first night at Szanto. Somehow, he had broken his indenture not long after Adolph arrived, and disap-

Adolph Zukor at the age of eighteen

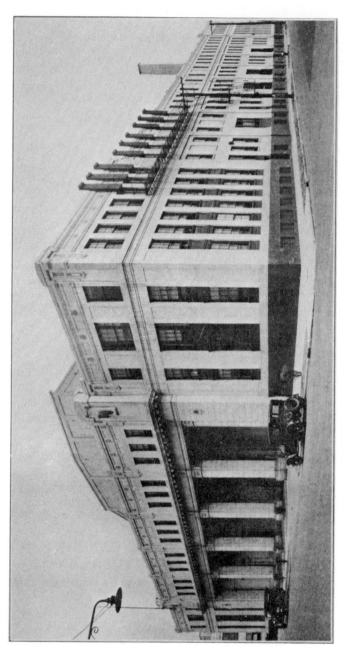

Paramount Famous Lasky Corporation's studio at Astoria, L. I.

peared from the region. They sat down on the front
stoop, exchanging greetings, views, and gossip.

Max had a job with a furrier; was learning the trade.
It was a great business with a future. Experts got salaries
as high as twenty-five dollars a week. Upholstery—what
kind of business was that? Thereupon, Adolph Zukor
told his troubles.

"I should say so!" replied Max Gross. "Now the fur
business is easy. You start in as errand boy and our shop
is full of Hungarians, so you don't have to know English. I'll tell you what I'll do—you come round next
Monday morning and I'll introduce you to the Boss.
His people and mine are cousins in the old country."

It was perhaps a gamble; but Adolph knew that he
could not long endure sofa-covering. He reported at the
upholstery shop on Monday morning only to hand in
his resignation, repaired to the factory of A. A. Frankel
at Mercer and Houston streets, lingered about the place
until the noon hour. Then he and Max invaded the
restaurant where the Boss was having luncheon and
presented their application. Without a break of a day,
Adolph Zukor went to work as errand boy—at four
dollars a week.

He swept the floor; he gathered up the leavings and
trimmings; he carried messages; he made himself generally useful. As his few words of English became rel-
atively intelligible, he passed down the work-benches
at lunch time, taking orders and collecting dimes.

Then he did business with a glassed-in lunch counter which protruded from the front of an old house in Houston Street. The cashier, when Adolph took away the last order, used to tip him a glass of milk and a sandwich or an apple and a piece of pie. And Adolph was a healthy sixteen-year-old boy, who could never eat too much!

After the busy season ended at Frankel's, he found that the house of Ederstrom, "Fur Novelties," in West Third Street, offered a better chance to learn the trade. So, still at four dollars a week, he began his third apprenticeship. With those deft hands of his, he went rapidly ahead. By 1891, when he stood on the verge of nineteen years, he was a full-fledged journeyman making the respectable wage of eight dollars a week.

When he got his job in the upholsterer's, Adolph left the flat of Gustavus Liebermann and went to board on Lewis Street in the heart of the East Side with the Seltzers, remote cousins from Ricse. They charged him three dollars a week; and he was making only two dollars. He supplied the difference from the little hoard in the lining of his second-best waistcoat. After he settled down into "furs," he boarded, at the same standard fee, with Mrs. Blau, daughter of the storekeeper to whom he was apprenticed at Szanto; she had married a cousin of the same name. Warm clothes against the New York winter had by now finished his treasured forty dollars.

The era of monotonous five-story tenements on the

East Side was only beginning. The Blau flat in Ninth
Street near Second Avenue occupied the floor of what
had been in the days of President Jackson a fine mansion; there was even a big back yard. Mr. Blau lived very
prettily on his salary as floorwalker for a Grand Street
department store. For Adolph's three dollars a week,
Mrs. Blau not only gave the little apprentice a clean
bed, breakfast, and dinner, but even a put-up luncheon.

He had small temptation for spending beyond these
bare necessities for he filled his days and nights with
hard work. To the immigrant, the English language
stands the first obstacle. This is especially true of the
Hungarian. Not that he lacks the gift of tongues; but
his native language is a world of philology away from
ours. Springing from a different stock, it "goes at
things" differently; our vowels, some of our consonants,
have no exact equivalent in Hungarian. Established in
the fur trade, Adolph Zukor entered a free public night
school in Stanton Street, and attended it somewhat
irregularly during a three-year residence in New York.
Here, he made acquaintance with the English classics.
His diamond-hard mind had always a trick of cutting
through the medium of expression to the idea beneath.
So Shakespeare and most of the other great English
poets went past him. Milton and Bunyan, however,
made a strong impression; perhaps his early rabbinical
education broke the ground for that. He still has his old
school copy of *Pilgrim's Progress;* and at intervals he

pores over it, trying to interpret it in terms of the screen.

"Read the newspapers," advised his teachers. With his alert interest in his new environment, he needed no such advice.

In those days, John L. Sullivan was in his glory. Adolph learned from the newspapers and the other apprentices what this glory meant. Boxing had become a craze with the boys of the East Side. One evening after work, Adolph put on the gloves in a corridor of the factory with another boy of about his own age and size. He got, of course, a fine trimming; and the rest of the apprentices laughed. Thereupon, he set himself to study the art. When his wages rose and he paid back his arrears of board to the Blaus, his first extravagance was a pair of boxing gloves. He practised constantly—in the corridors of the factory, in the back yard of the Blau house on Ninth Street, even in Tompkins Square near by. He was in that flyweight class not yet recognized by the authorities; always he must box with bigger boys, making up with agility, speed, and cleverness what he lacked in bulk.

One of his opponents had a pretty trick which Adolph much admired. Instead of parrying blows always with his gloves—as was then the crude fashion—he twisted his head sidewise and let his opponent's fist go harmlessly past his ear. Adolph practised that trick, and the appropriate, useful counter to the face. Having no expert instructor, he formed the habit of ducking always to the right. In a year or so he had started a beautiful cauliflower on his left ear. Years later, when appearances began to have their uses in his life, the surgeons did their best to prune it down; but that ear still has a curious, flattened extension.

The fur business was seasonal in those days; fashion had not yet conceived the "summer fur." Its busy season began in May and it slackened off nothing before Christmas. The journeymen and apprentices had to find other employment for the winter and early spring. Most of the other apprentices worked during the slack season at bottling imported wine. So when Frankel laid off its force, Adolph busied himself with piece-work, which amounted to three or four dollars a week, in a wine cellar on Third Avenue. There were other ways of supplementing a small income. Ridley's Department Store in Grand Street needed extra packers and wrappers on Saturday night. Beginners earned twenty-five cents; experts, fifty cents. Mr. Blau got him a regular Saturday night job at Ridley's. Some of the other boys in his amorphic boxing club earned twenty or fifty cents a night as supers in the melodramas along the Bowery. Fascinated by the glitter of the footlights, Adolph applied once at the stage door of the London Theatre. But the stage manager threw him out of line—he was too small for the drama.

For the rest, American life as he lived it was that of the Tompkins Square gang. They emphasized masculine values. No mediæval monks regarded woman with more superiority and contempt. To appear on the streets with a girl was a sign of deplorable weakness; at the sight of a skirt, one closed his eyes and stilled his fluttering heart. When at last a member of the gang "got struck on a girl," he signed his decree of banishment from self-respecting masculine society. The only women in Adolph Zukor's life were Mrs. Blau and his elderly female relatives.

Sometimes the Blaus went picnicking on Sundays in Prospect Park, Brooklyn. This involved a journey of two or three hours by horse car or on foot; and it seemed to the boy of Tompkins Square like a trek into the remote wilderness. He went along only for politeness; his heart was back with the gang, boxing in the back yards. In that period, woods and trees and the out-of-doors called up only boresome memories of Ricse with its dead, unambitious atmosphere.

He was drinking the life of the East Side pavements in great gulps; loving it, happy in it. "The cheerfulest boy I ever knew," says Max Schosberg, who worked at the next bench. "Always singing Hungarian songs. Music is all right in its place, understand me, but I told him many times to shut up."

For once, Adolph Zukor of the creative will was drifting on the surface of life. This same Max Schosberg relit the fire. A year or so before Adolph, he had landed at Castle Garden from Vaszar, Hungary. He was therefore a little more advanced in his knowledge of America and the fur business. "It's a good trade," said Max, "but what is a trade? Get in business for yourself, I say." As soon as he learned enough English, Max hoped to take up salesmanship. And presently he had an idea.

The house of Ederstrom made "novelties"—small pieces like stoles, ties, and trimmings. He bought a new pelt or two which he and Adolph, working after hours in the factory or in their rooms, transformed into fur scarves. Max peddled the finished product among the small East Side merchants and sold them all. He and Adolph divided ten dollars as first profit in this transaction. As soon as he became a journeyman, Adolph Zukor had opened an account in the Dry Dock Savings Bank. Now he drew on it for capital to buy more furs. Then Max wheedled out of an East Side fur shop an order which amounted to a contract. They had insufficient money to buy raw furs for an enterprise so ambitious. Adolph thereupon borrowed $140 from Blau, his landlord, and got the loan of a vacant room in the apartment above as a workshop. In the busy season of 1891, Adolph worked constantly until midnight; and his profits from this little whirl at business far exceeded his wages.

Max, however, grew restless. He had friends in Chicago. They wrote that the fur business was just getting a start there, Max saw a better opportunity than in New York. In the slack season of 1891-92, he pulled up stakes and travelled westward.

With his partner gone, Adolph felt a stirring of new adventure. Chicago was working up to the great Columbian Exposition of 1893. Stories of the preparations filled the newspapers. Adolph wanted mightily to see it. Passing down Broadway one afternoon, a sign advertising cut-rate tickets to Chicago caught his eye. On impulse, he went in and inquired the price. It was less than he thought. Next week he had resigned from Ederstrom's, closed up his affairs, packed, drawn his account in full from the Dry Dock Savings Bank, and in a crawling day coach started his second journey into the world. He was then nineteen.

BOOK II

STRUGGLE

CHAPTER IV

NOVELTY FURS

CHICAGO, with the wild Northwest at her doors, had begun existence as a trading post for furs. It remained an important centre for the traffic in raw pelts. However, New York, fashion centre for the country, had appropriated to herself the business of working furs into coats, boas, muffs, and trimmings. Chicago was struggling to establish herself as a competitor. This budding industry stood housed in rows of old buildings along the river.

When he had unpacked his trunk in a Hungarian boarding house, Adolph Zukor walked to the fur district and made the rounds, looking for a job. His stature made him seem even younger than his years. That counted against him. On the other hand, he had special goods to sell. Until a year or so before, women had dressed their throats in winter with simple boas. Then Paris or Leipzig sprung a new idea. Taking the pelt of any small, long animal—at first always a mink—the fur worker dressed it with the tail and front legs intact, and affixed a stuffed head whose beady eyes seemed to glare reproach at its murderers. That was to be one of the longest-lived fancies in modern fashion; it is going yet.

Just at the period when Adolph Zukor became a full-fledged journeyman, the mink scarf burst on New York like an explosion. Ederstrom had seen the opportunity, and during the last six months in New York Adolph Zukor did little else than make this new confection. Fashions travelled westward rather slowly in those days; the rage for mink scarves had just begun to manifest itself in Chicago. Workmen who knew the trick were in demand. In three different establishments, Adolph got a hearing and a chance to demonstrate his skill. All of them offered him a place. He chose the one which seemed to afford the best prospects, and went to work next morning. In negotiating for the job, he had neglected to ask one important question—the amount of his weekly wage. He thought it most diplomatic to make no present inquiries. When his fortnightly pay envelope came, it held twenty-four dollars. By moving to Chicago, he had raised his wages four dollars a week!

However, he worked at that bench less than a month. For in the meantime, he had found Max Schosberg. And Max raved over the commercial opportunities of Chicago. Already the World's Fair had started a boom. Also, fur scarves were going to be a rage that season, a furore.

"Let's set up in business for ourselves," said Max, "you make the stuff and I sell it—same as we did in New York."

Between them, they had a few hundred dollars of

savings. That would buy pelts enough for a start. Further, Max had learned some things about American business. "Those banks, now," he said; "when they see a young fellow is bound to get ahead, they will lend him money just on his note."

The restless and courageous Adolph needed little persuading. Within a week—for they must strike while the fur season was on and the scarf still a novelty—they had rented a single room in La Salle Street, installed a hired sewing machine, employed an operator, and gone to work. The young partners made up a few dozen sample scarves. Max carried them forth on his shoulder. They sold on sight. Before the season ended, their Novelty Fur Company made for both Max and Adolph a thousand dollars over and above living expenses.

The slack season of 1893 gave Adolph Zukor the leisure to visit the World's Fair. In a little side-show tent of the Midway Plaisance flourished the first moving-picture show which ever charged admission to the public; a crude affair. The perfected moving-picture machine of to-day is the compound of many inventions, the life work of many inventors. In 1889, however, Thomas A. Edison had by one of his simple genius-touches made practicable the apparatus for taking the photographs, and had carried projection to the point where he could show the image through a glass slide. Projection onto a screen remained only a hazy dream. By 1892, he prepared to manufacture commercially his kinetoscope. This device for showing the pictures consisted of a high box like a fat pillar, into which the spectator looked through a peep-hole. So postured, he beheld, seemingly on a glass plate, a girl doing the skirt dance or a man making realistic gestures. Edison intended to exhibit the kinetoscope at the World's Fair. However, a hitch in manufacturing prevented that. Now among the by-paths which branched from the main road of this invention was the Anchnitz tachyscope, a device even less perfected than the kinetoscope. When its owners found that Edison could not get ready in time, they set up shop at the Fair. This, too, was a peep-show device. Its star actor was an elephant, which walked glimmeringly across the tiny field of vision. That was wonder enough!

I should like to record that young Adolph Zukor saw this exhibition and stood thrilled; that the five-cent piece he gave up at the door was the initial investment which grew into his present fortune. In sober truth, he cannot remember whether he saw the tachyscope or no. Probably he did not. He had heard of the moving picture—yes. However, this America was an exciting new world, full of wonders. . . .

Besides, when spring came to Chicago he had found a new interest. The original White Sox were in their glory; the town had gone mad over baseball. The boys in Tompkins Square made a god of John L. Sullivan. The clothing operatives and apprentice clerks in his Hungarian boarding house worshipped that less rugged hero, "Pop" Anson. In Tompkins Square, Adolph had learned the Yankee art of throwing and catching; but he had never played in a regular game. Now, he took with enthusiasm to vacant-lot baseball.

Perhaps it expresses his courage and ambition that he chose the hardest position for a man of his pounds and inches—catcher. In those days, catching was catching. The big mitt or "pud" had just arrived; but the vacant-lot teams considered this protection cowardly and effeminate. The catcher trusted to the protection of a skimpy mask over his face and a skin-tight, fingerless glove on the left hand. Adolph developed a good peg to second, and became a Machiavelli at working the pitcher for a base on balls. Then one day a foul tip caught him on the little finger of the right hand, bending it L-shaped. Maturity straightened it out a little, but it is still crooked. His deft hands formed the best part of his working capital; he dared not risk them further. So he transferred himself to second base, and found it a position better suited to a man of his size and agility. Of summer afternoons, he sat sometimes on the bleachers, joining in the popular adoration of "Pop" Anson and King Kelly.

As soon as they opened the Novelty Fur Company, the partners found one great flaw in their business equipment. They were still deficient in conversational English. With retailers who spoke Hungarian and Yiddish, Max Schosberg got along splendidly. But when his customer was an Irishman or a Yankee. . . . "They just laugh at me!" complained Max.

Adolph compared the colloquial English he had acquired from the gang in Tompkins Square with the rules of grammar he had learned in night school. They did not match at all. Facing the problem squarely, he, Max, and another young Hungarian employed a tutor and spent their evenings in vocal gymnastics. Adolph Zukor lacks the language faculty. Also, naturally and by training his mind goes straight to the heart of a matter, extracting the gold, rejecting the slag. To such a mind the mode of expression is a mere extraneous detail. But since other people set store by this accomplishment, let us acquire it. Through many years to come, he was to keep up the struggle with our baffling language. Now, in his eloquent moment he hits the idea dead-centre with the divinely appropriate English word. But coaching and practice have never quite brushed away his native Hungarian accent.

With the opening of the busy season in 1893, the Novelty Fur Company went ahead to a startling minor success. Chicago had proved a fortunate location. The famous financial depression blighted business over the rest of America, but the Fair kept Chicago going. Just as the partners had calculated, tourists and sightseers from the small towns made their visit to the Fair an excuse to do some metropolitan shopping. The demand for mink scarves continued; and Adolph Zukor—Max used to introduce him as "superintendent of our mechanical department"—made the best in Chicago.

Even before the end of their first year, they had taken on extra hands. Now they employed a working force of twenty-five men. Adolph designed some fancies of his own. These sold, but nothing went so well as his mink scarves. The Novelty Fur Company, it seemed, held the world in its grasp. If they could do this in Chicago, why not elsewhere? Adolph Zukor's native ambition sprang fully awake. He imagined a string of establishments running from coast to coast. As a beginning, the Novelty Fur Company opened a branch in Peoria. When the rush season ended, Adolph was pale and thin with work and thinking; but he had in the bank eight thousand dollars, cold cash.

There was more yet to come. He and Max Schosberg had overlooked the trimmings and leavings of their pelts. Hatters buy these as raw material for the "topper." The partners gathered up this accumulation, and Max bargained so shrewdly that they divided twelve hundred dollars.

Now Max had left a mother in Hungary. Like many European mothers, she conceived of America in dime-novel terms. Cowboys, bandits, and Indians rode the streets, shooting at you. Bears and rattlesnakes bit you. Max wrote, to no avail, that Chicago was a fine orderly city like Budapest. Mrs. Schosberg set that down as kindly but false reassurance. Her latest letter had betrayed intense mental depression.

"I'm going to use my share from the trimmings for a visit to Mother," said Max.

This put an idea into Adolph's head. Since he apprenticed himself to the storekeeper at Szanto, he had never taken a real vacation. And the future seemed secure. "I'll go along!" he announced.

By the cheapest possible modes of conveyance, they travelled to Budapest. There they separated. Adolph Zukor went to Ricse, renewed childhood acquaintances, basked in the aura of his success, got first-hand news of his brother Arthur. This brilliant young cleric had attracted so much attention by his learning and eloquence that Berlin proposed to keep him. He stood on the threshold of his great career as a liberal rabbi; and all Jewish Ricse expected of him what he afterward fulfilled. Adolph drifted back by way of Paris and London, where he stopped to see the sights; and, as the busy season approached, he reached Chicago a little in advance of Max Schosberg.

The stimulant of a World's Fair had exhausted its effect; the Lake Region was beginning to feel those prolonged and desperate hard times. Also, the Novelty Fur Company had lost its old leadership in mink scarves; its greater competitors had learned the trick. And while the partners felt round for a saleable novelty to take its place, Max had more bad news. His mother had fallen ill. Part of the trouble was her anxiety over him. Max must return to Hungary.

The Dual Monarchy was working up to that intensive armament which, for two decades before the explosion, turned Europe into an armed camp. When Max and Adolph made their vacation visit, Hungarian subjects who had emigrated before they were seventeen stood exempt from military service. Now, Hungary suddenly revoked that exception. The apparitors of Franz Josef gathered in Max Schosberg. For the time being, Adolph Zukor must needs go it alone.

To finish this part of the business: by 1896, when Max Schosberg could return to Chicago, the Novelty Fur Company had fallen to the depths and was working back toward prosperity. Adolph Zukor, in the course of the struggle, had developed new tastes. He liked "outside work"—dealing with customers and wholesale houses. To sit in the back room directing the operatives contented him no longer. Also, Max thought he saw a golden opportunity in Peoria. So they dissolved partnership, Adolph keeping the Chicago business and Max the Peoria branch. They were never associated again, though they remained personal friends to the end of the chapter. Max Schosberg went on to a comfortable fortune; he is now manager of the fur department at Gimbel's, New York. "But I wish I had stayed with Adolph," he says.

Alone, his own salesman and factory manager, Adolph Zukor found the sensational specialty for which he had been looking. That was the period of balloon sleeves; and Paris had put forth the short fur "shoulder cape," which was selling furiously in New York. Modern illustrators, portraying or caricaturing the 'nineties, love to hang this garment on the ladies of their pictures; it had a touch of the chic and another of the ridiculous. The top of it clasped over the high choker collar then in fashion; thence it flared out just to the outer and upper corner of the exaggerated sleeves. In front it curved like a bib across the collarbone. Adolph Zukor experimented with the new style until he got the trick. The first samples had a ready sale. His next partner said of him in after years: "Adolph was always in too much of a hurry." Having picked the fur cape as his winning specialty, he gambled all the resources of the Novelty Fur Company. Going still further, he borrowed from the bank to the limit of his credit.

It was a short-lived fashion. Before Adolph Zukor really started, the vogue was dying out in New York. Chicago took it up only to drop it abruptly. Adolph Zukor ended his first season as sole manager of the Novelty Fur Company with a storehouseful of dead stock and a staggering burden of debts. "Go into bankruptcy," advised some of his elders. But he shut that trap of a mouth and shook his head. It was not an honest way out; it would be a black spot on his record.

Those were hard times, when backers pressed lightly on debtors; the bank agreed to give him a little time òn his notes. He travelled from creditor to creditor, persuading them their best chance of getting their money back was to let him go on. The fur business of Chicago had regarded with indulgent interest the enterprise of those two stripling boys, Schosberg and Zukor. Now that the rocket had come down like a stick, "ladies' furs" retained some of its indulgence; Zukor found that he had friends. He lived small through the slack season, and schemed.

Meantime, having completed five years of American residence and come of age, he took out his naturalization papers. In 1896, the Democratic National Convention met in Chicago, and William Jennings Bryan stampeded it to free silver by his famous cross-of-gold speech. Adolph Zukor had that day found a seat in the gallery of the Coliseum. He heard it, every word. "Bunk!" he said, and cast his vote for McKinley. He has voted Republican ever since.

CHAPTER V

THE SOD HOUSE

$\mathcal{N}$ow we will leave Adolph Zukor at the end of his first defeat—struggling with debts and with the temptation to take the easy path of bankruptcy. We must go back a decade and trace another thread of life which that magical Penny Arcade was to transmute into golden wire.

In 1881, the two Kohn boys, Morris and Samuel, emigrated to the United States. Their origins and background resembled those of Adolph Zukor. They were born and reared in Erdö Benye, another little town of the Tokay wine district in Hungary. Time out of mind the Kohns had enjoyed modest prosperity as wine-growers and wine-makers. In the late 'seventies that American plague phyloxera began devastating the French vineyards. Irresistibly, it marched eastward to blight the Tokay district. One year the Kohns pressed and sold their vintage as usual. The next, both crop and vines were a smudgy tangle of diseased pulp and wood. Even before this calamity, letters from emigrant relatives had fired the young imaginations of Morris and Samuel with the opportunities of America. On the proceeds of a small inheritance, they took steerage and emigrant train, and landed in Chicago with less than ten dollars between them.

One Beifeld, a Hungarian, had founded years before a pioneer cloak factory. The establishment remained as Hungarian as Szamarodni wine. There the Kohn boys got a job and set about learning the trade. They had left in Hungary their elder sister Esther, married to a vineyard owner named Herman Kaufmann. He, also, had lost his modest all in the phyloxera epidemic. "All for one and one for all" was the family motto. The brothers lived small and sent their savings back to Hungary. A year later, the Kaufmann family, including their young children, came to Chicago. Morris Kohn, always the active and enterprising intelligence of the family, had a job waiting for Herman Kaufmann. He became a suit-presser at Beifeld's.

Still peasant by instinct, the Kohns had the peasant hunger for land. The American custom of giving away virgin tracts to all comers burst upon them with the dazzle of a fairy tale. Just then Dakota—still a territory and still undivided—had entered the initial stages of American progress. It was enjoying a temporary boom, stimulated by the railroads. A few years afterward the boom collapsed, and the Dakotas built on the wreckage their permanent and sober prosperity. That is the American way. The Kohn boys had entered night school and begun to acquire English. Strolling one night in the downtown district, Morris Kohn puzzled out a sign advertising the bonanza crops, the unlimited possibilities and, above all, the free lands of undeveloped northern Dakota. He entered, had a talk with the land agent and emerged in a state of dazzled enthusiasm. For a mere registration fee, the government would give any bona-fide settler one hundred and sixty acres. He himself could take up one of these quarter sections. So could Sam and Herman and Mrs. Kaufmann, making a ranch of six hundred and forty acres in all. That, in Hungarian terms, meant the acreage of a great lord.

For a winter the Kohns and Kaufmanns worked and saved and dreamed. By March, 1884, they had between them exactly three hundred and eighty dollars. In the horse market over by the stockyards, they purchased the outfit of a discouraged immigrant—a rickety covered wagon, a set of mended harness, and three scrubby broncos.

The railroad, by way of encouraging settlers, would rent a box car to Devil's Lake—the northern terminus—for sixty dollars. Rapid calculation proved this a cheaper way than driving the team. The firm of Kohn and Kaufmann hired a car and loaded aboard the horses, the wagon, and every stick of household furniture which they could spare from Chicago. So, travelling free as horse-traders, Morris Kohn and Herman Kaufmann started on the great adventure. Samuel, Mrs. Kaufmann, and the children were for the present to remain in Chicago, living on Samuel's wages as a

clothing operative. The journey took a week, during
which the two young adventurers slept shivering on hay
and ate cold meals. They were young, however, and to
boys who knew only the manicured fields of Hungary or
the smoky walls of Chicago, these wide, wind-blown skies
and unlimited surges of rolling land afforded every
hour a new and thrilling interest. When more than
forty years later Morris Kohn told me the story of
this adventure, he remembered not so much its hard-
ships as its glories. The green shoots of April were just
beginning to tinge the northern prairies when they
pulled into Devil's Lake. "It looked like a frontier
town in the movies," says Morris Kohn.

Devil's Lake was up to its neck in the land boom.
The crowd about the general store welcomed the
young adventurers as advance guard of a horde which
before snow flew would make their desert blossom
like the rose. Even Kohn and Kaufmann's halting,
broken English appealed at the moment not to the rough
Western sense of humour, but to the hearty Western
admiration for courage and enterprise. An old settler
stepped forward and offered to guide them to a good
fertile location which no one had as yet staked out.
After a hurried consultation in Hungarian, Morris and
Herman decided to take a chance and accept. They
bought at the general store the lumber and tar paper
for a "shack." Their guide mounted, led them twenty
miles northward, stopped, and pointed to a beautiful

stretch of rolling prairie land traversed by a water
course. Morris mounted and rode over it. His horse's
hoofs threw up black richness. "Here we stay!" he
said. Before they went to bed in the immigrant wagon
they had found the government markers which designated the first of their four quarter-sections.

Next morning they set themselves to put up their
shack. Morris loved mechanics; he had been looking
forward to that. They had staked out the horses to spare
timbers and let them graze. But spring in South Dakota
was more backward than they thought. The new shoots of
grass made poor pickings. So at about noon Herman
Kaufmann mounted, rode three miles to the nearest
habitation, and bought a load of hay for immediate
delivery. Just at dusk, when they were nailing into
place the last length of tar paper, the hay arrived.

Now they had in their string a half-broken bronco
with a talent for trouble. When the hay wagon came
creaking over the hill he took that excuse to snort, rear,
and bolt, dragging the timber. His tether pulled loose.
And the other horses caught the contagion as horses
will. They, too, pulled their ropes loose from the timbers.
Morris and Herman ran after them. The horses coquet-
ted with their pursuers, stopping to graze, and then
when the chase came close, galloping away again. So it
went, mile after mile across the trackless prairie while
a clear, dark night settled down and a cold wind, spring-

ing up from the north, stabbed the throats and arms of the two young adventurers—for they had been working in their shirt sleeves. At last they glimpsed a light in the distance. Morris and Herman managed to start a stampede in that direction. The horses stopped under a haystack; but when the pursuers approached them with fair words, they still shied and ran. Morris groped his way to the farmhouse, threw himself on the mercies of the farmer. This experienced Westerner tried to catch the runaways, and failed as dismally as the two greenhorns. Finally, he turned his own horses out to feed on the haystack. That quieted the Kaufmann-Kohn broncos; he laid hands on them at last. Morris interviewed the farmer on the lay of the land. He recognized their location; they were about ten miles from home.

They mounted two of the horses bareback, guiding them by looped halters, and led the other. The night was turning bitterly cold, and they were still in their shirt sleeves. Having learned their horsemanship in temperate Hungary, they underestimated the hardihood of the Western bronco; through chattering teeth, Morris and Herman exchanged their fears that the horses would freeze their legs. So they travelled for hours, but no shape of a hill in the darkness seemed to resemble their quarter-section. It grew colder. Morris remembered seeing buffalo wallows all over the region; these would afford some shelter against that nipping wind. Leaving Herman to hold the horses, he went exploring—and pitched over the edge of a wallow not a hundred yards away. Into this they led the horses and trotted solemnly round and round all night. At the first streak of dawn Morris climbed the nearest hill for an observation. Two or three miles away he spied the shack and barn of a nester. Thither they rode. Roused, this settler gave their horses room in his warm barn, bedded down the partners for a two-hour sleep before his fire, shared his morning coffee.

"Well, nothing much happened that afternoon," says Morris Kohn. "But next day—what a day!" The partners were unpacking, setting things to rights. While Morris started experiments with clearing land, Herman made the cabin shipshape. A tin of kerosene had spilled into their metal water pail. Herman, by way of cleaning it out, set the inside of the pail afire, and poured out the burning mixture onto the ground. It ignited last year's dry grass. In two minutes the prairie was on fire. Morris, summoned by his partner's yells, joined in the fight to put it out. It was too late. And the wind was carrying it down onto their shack—already the tar paper had caught fire. Seizing the axe and sledge, they knocked their frail habitation to pieces and threw the boards and timbers across the line of flame to the unburned windward area. That sinister plume of smoke attracted the attention of the experienced neighbour three miles away. He rode to join them. But the fire had a start by now; it seemed that the whole prairie was gone. They had abandoned hope when rain began to fall. It turned in an hour to snow, to a belated blizzard.

Now that the weather had intervened to save him, the neighbour took the adventures of the greenhorns as a joke and offered them a haven for the night in his barn. Next morning Morris and Herman drove through the snow to Devil's Lake, bought more tar paper, and incidentally filed their claims. Then they rebuilt the shack.

After this lively first week, there were no more accidents or incidents. They built a sod house in the side of a hill, broke forty acres, and planted it in potatoes. The bank, they found, was lending money to bona-fide settlers. So they went into debt for the price of agricultural machinery and a cow. In the late summer Mrs. Kaufmann and the children came on from Chicago. The potatoes, the cow, and Samuel's steady remittances kept them alive through that winter.

Meantime, Morris Kohn found a way to supplement the family income. All this time, Indians were drifting back and forth down the trails, bringing furs; Morris mentioned this fact in his letters to Samuel. Thereupon Samuel and a friend in the fur trade raised a little money and sent it to Morris, together with some expert information on qualities and prices. Through a temperature that sank sometimes to ten degrees below zero, Morris drove their single farm wagon into the Turtle

Mountains and, sleeping in tepees or in the wagon-bed, trafficked with the Indians and the half-breed trappers. He bought red fox pelt, muskrat hides, bear-skins. His modest profits helped in the purchase of ploughs, harrows, tools, and domestic supplies.

This transaction is like the first moment of impulse in a drama. Unconsciously, Morris Kohn had entered the fur business. That would lead as by magic guidance to his meeting with Adolph Zukor, to the Penny Arcade in New York and the transformation of the moving picture. . . .

CHAPTER VI

BACK TO CHICAGO

*A*s soon as the frost was out of the ground, Morris and Herman began working sixteen hours a day at breaking land. Those two inexperienced men alone accomplished that season the superhuman task of planting nearly a quarter-section in wheat. Under the suns and rains of a good crop year, it flourished mightily. The stalks grew as high as a man's shoulder, and they were "heading up" to plump richness. The partners sat in the sod house by night, figuring in the illumination of a guttering candle. The profits would set them more than even with the world. Next year they would plant the whole section. It was a bonanza!

And in the first week of August, down from the Arctic came a premature frost. It blasted the wheat; turned the golden ears to filthy black pellets. . . .

They stood the blow as best they could. Samuel kept up his remittances from Chicago. But interest and pressing debts used up all that money, and the family in the sod house must live. Morris went out to find work for the winter. A company of gentleman farmers from Canada had taken up an area near by and begun an ambitious programme of building. They employed Morris as a carpenter and, when his talent with tools became manifest, paid him the usual wages of thirty dollars a month and board. After the northern frosts made carpentry impossible, he did a little more trading with the Indians in the Turtle Mountains, and acquired a little more education in furs. Next year, the partners broke no more land. That would take money; and they had reached the end of their credit. They harvested part of a crop. But the profit just carried them through the winter; they were not gaining on the debt. And the premature North Dakota boom, punctured by that early frost of the year before, was beginning to collapse. Morris Kohn took stock with himself. This promised to be a long struggle. He could make more immediate money in Chicago than in Dakota; and it was the American city rather than the American country which offered chances to an ambitious boy. He and Herman Kaufmann saw their creditors in Devil's Lake and got promise of more time on accounts and notes.

Next week, Morris Kohn was back at his machine in Beifeld's factory. He told his tale to the Boss, who admired the pluck of the performance. "How much do you and Herman owe up there?" asked Beifeld. Morris Kohn told him. "All right," said the Boss, "I'll pay your debts, and you can give me a third of your wages until you've cleared it off." On these terms, Morris Kohn retired from the business of farming.

That is the story as Morris Kohn tells it. The Kaufmann side of this epic is more picturesque and more tragic. One of the little boys died in that sod house by the water hole; the baby, nineteen months old. He developed convulsions. Herman, riding like mad across the prairie, was sixteen hours in finding the doctor and twelve hours more in getting him to the claim. At that, the doctor was drunk. "But he was just as good drunk as sober," says one of the Kaufmanns cryptically. When he arrived, the baby was dead. Herman and Morris made a coffin out of pine boards and Mrs. Kaufmann sewed a shroud. They laid him away at the summit of their hill. Their little private graveyard, they have heard since, has become the Jewish burying ground for that region of North Dakota. During the six years of the Kaufmann tenure on this pioneer farm, Mrs. Kaufmann gave birth to two babies, Al and Julie. They appeared before Herman could bring the midwife from Devil's Lake.

Other episodes have a livelier colour. Mrs. Kaufmann was no sooner settled in the sod house than a band of Sioux Indians squatted in a ring about the door. Silent, with intent beady eyes, they watched her cooking. The men were out of calling distance. Taking the only means she could think of to avert a massacre, Mrs. Kaufmann gave them a batch of fresh cookies. They ate, grunted, rose, departed. More Indians came. Always the terrified Mrs. Kaufmann fed them; and always they departed in peace. Whenever she saw the dust of dragging tepee poles down the road, she rushed to the stove and started a fire. But next spring, when the Indians came out of winter quarters for their hunting, that original band stopped at her door and with cordial grunts gave her a freshly killed antelope and some skins to wrap her babies in—present for present. Then she began better to understand them; even to like them.

Once, after she had fed a band of these self-invited guests, a squaw lingered behind. She did not seem well. Mrs. Kaufmann gave her a cup of hot tea. She thanked her hostess with her eyes, rose, disappeared in the direction of the barn. Mrs. Kaufmann supposed that she had gone. But an hour later she reëntered, carrying in her blanket a new-born papoose. She accepted another cup of tea, picked up her baby, and hurried on after the train. . . .

One night three men rode up with a fusilade of hoofs, knocked imperatively at the door, and asked for food. Her men were away. Mrs. Kaufmann, shaking with terror, cooked coffee and bacon. Two of the invaders ate at the table, and then one carried his rations to a third who stayed outside riding herd on a band of horses. They offered to pay. Mrs. Kaufmann, who had learned frontier manners, refused the money. They laid it emphatically on the table, rose, and drove the horses away. At dawn, another knocking at the door. This time the front yard was filled with mounted and armed men who demanded to know if any strangers had come that way. Her midnight guests were horse thieves, making their way with a stolen band to the safety of the Canadian border. Mrs. Kaufmann was glad to learn, a week later, that they had made their escape, for she had seen in the hands of the posse the noosed rope, all greased and ready. . . .

The Kaufmanns acquired a little string of cattle. Ninna and Lottie, the two eldest, were now lively little grigs, playing dolls with the Indian girls and riding like vaqueros. There were nights when the temperature fell to thirty degrees below zero and the earth snapped with sharp explosions and the cattle drifted before the blizzard wind. Ninna and Lottie would ride forth to round up the herd and drive it to shelter while Mrs. Kaufmann guided them by swinging a lantern on the end of a pole.

Four or five years of this, and the Kaufmanns took stock. . . . They had the section broken now; possessed barns and machinery. But the girls were growing up; all winter the two eldest rode ten miles to school on the same bronco. This was the consideration that drew the Kaufmanns finally from North Dakota. Her experience with the horse rustlers had shown Mrs. Kaufmann what kind of characters haunted those frontier roads. Also the Indians, finding their hunting grounds invaded and ruined, were growing sullen. Hours before Ninna and Lottie came loping over the crest of their hill in the afternoon shadows, Mrs.

Kaufmann found herself straining her eyes at the horizon. She and Herman Kaufmann pondered on other things. All her daughters were growing up beautiful; they would marry some day, of course. And into what? ... farm drudgery. ...

So after six years of rough pioneering, the Kaufmanns pulled up stakes and moved back to Chicago, where Herman reëntered the clothing business. They had three daughters by now. Two of them, Ninna and Lottie, were born in Hungary; Julie had first seen the light in that sod house. Frances, the baby of the family, came after they moved back to the city. All these daughters were to marry well—exceptionally well —giving their pioneer mother a serene and happy old age. Of their two remaining sons, the eldest died soon after their removal. But Al Kaufmann survived to enter the nobility of the moving picture.

Meantime, Morris Kohn had climbed out of the ruck. At about the time when he finished paying off his debt to Beifeld, he turned his attention to the cumbersome cutting machine with which his shop formed the raw shapes of men's garments. It was an unsatisfactory instrument. Morris glowed always to mechanics. Stitching at his table, he conceived a revolutionary improvement. With his first savings, he got his device patented. Tried out at Beifeld's, it worked beautifully. Raising a little capital on his prospects, Morris Kohn journeyed to New York and put his invention on the market.

Scarcely had he made his first sale, when he discovered that another clothing worker had patented an attachment better and more practical than his own. This rival, however, was holding out for high prices. Morris shrewdly adopted the contrary policy—quick sales and small profits while the bonanza lasted. When business slowed up, he sold his rights, returned to Chicago, invested his winnings in the clothing industry. But his early trading among the Sioux had given him an instinct for furs and some training in assessing the quality of pelts. Inevitably, perhaps, he drifted toward that business. Ten years after he abandoned the homestead in South Dakota, he had become a highly successful broker in raw furs, dealing not only with Chicago but with New York, St. Louis, the Northwest, and even London. Meantime, he had married a sister of Emil Shauer, who will figure later as a character in this story.

CHAPTER VII

A MARRIAGE AND A
PARTNERSHIP

GENERALLY, his male acquaintances of old years cannot remember when or where they first met Adolph Zukor. He was so insignificant of stature, so reserved of manner, that the beholder paid him only passive attention—until some flash of shrewd insight or of common sense awoke the realization that here stood a man. With women, I fancy, it was different. For his face was virile but comely; now, when he has passed fifty, it retains in some aspects a great beauty. Even his cameo of a figure must have appealed to the mother in them. However, Adolph Zukor, in the year when he stood to his neck in debts of the vanished Novelty Fur Company, was not interested in the ladies. He still held the attitude of the Tompkins Square gang. After a hard week of struggle with his perplexities, he spent Saturday and Sunday hopping round second base; on one side of his nature prematurely a man of affairs and on the other, still a boy.

The first meeting between him and Morris Kohn remains an exception to this rule. Morris remembers it vividly. Keeping touch with the gossip of the fur business as a broker must, he had heard of those two mere boys, Schosberg and Zukor, who had built up that successful little Novelty Fur Company and gone aground on the reefs of the shoulder cape. Kohn did not take the temporary embarrassment seriously; he understood that a business dealing with the caprices of fashion has its necessary ups and downs, its spectacular losses and gains. So when a customer offered one day to bring in Adolph Zukor and introduce him, Morris Kohn listened.

"I don't want to do business with him, of course," said Morris Kohn; "I'm playing for the big fellows, not the small fry. But fetch him along. I'd like to have a look at him."

Zukor had not sat for five minutes in the office before Morris Kohn, who thinks largely and widely himself, began to recognize a kindred spirit. In half an hour, Zukor was confessing his ragged financial condition. In an hour, Morris Kohn, remembering the lift that Beifeld had given him when he himself came back from North Dakota loaded with debts, was jotting down figures on a scratch pad. Kohn knew of odd contracts available for that little, distressed factory down in Market Street. Also, there were means of liquidating some of the dead stock. This sensible and plucky youth who refused to take the easy way of bankruptcy appealed more and more to Morris Kohn. When they parted, he found that he had laid out a whole plan of campaign.

On an upper floor of the building where Kohn displayed his pelts, flourished a dealer in odd lots. Kohn knew nothing ill of him. At Kohn's suggestion, this man took over some of Zukor's stock and arranged to dispose of it on commission. A few days later, Adolph Zukor came into Kohn's office with all his temper blazing—in a murderous mood. A friend had revealed to him the situation in that storehouse up above. The odd-lot broker was crooked. He intended, apparently, to sell off Zukor's stock, pocket all the receipts, and trust to the principle that possession is nine points of the law. Only that week he had sold three hundred and eighty-five dollars' worth of these goods; and when Adolph had asked for an accounting, he had reported "no sales."

Morris Kohn called up a few acquaintances on the telephone, asked some pointed questions. He had leaped before he looked; the man had a slippery reputation. Adolph Zukor, raging in the corner, was alternately for physical violence and for going to the law.

"It will do you no good to beat him up," said Morris Kohn, "and a lawsuit will cost you more than they're worth. I have an idea."

Ignatz, the office boy in that crooked loft above, had worked for Morris Kohn, owed him a good turn. Morris Kohn lingered in the hall until Ignatz came downstairs.

"Kid," he said, "would you mind staying round your

shop for an hour or so after the boss goes home? I may want to call to-night—but don't tell him that."

The shrewd Ignatz, it appeared, had perceived the true nature of that business upstairs, and was getting ready to resign. He needed but little persuasion. As soon as the proprietor was safely gone, Morris Kohn and Adolph Zukor invaded the establishment. An expert in precious stones can tell every diamond in the world from every other. A trained shepherd can pick out, from a bunch of three thousand, any sheep at which he has once taken a good look. By that same trade sense, the fur man knows any individual pelt or piece. Adolph Zukor went through the loft identifying his own stock. He, Morris Kohn, and Ignatz gathered it up, carried it down to Kohn's wareroom. Adolph counted and calculated. There was missing exactly three hundred and eighty-five dollars' worth. The odd-lot broker had made only the one sale.

Next morning Kohn and Zukor came early to the office. They heard the broker mount the stairs, heard him burst into the hall yelling that he had been robbed. "No, you haven't," cried Morris Kohn. "Come here!"

A third of a century later, Morris Kohn told me the rest of the story.

"Well, we were both young fellows," he said, "and young fellows like the rough stuff. I backed him into the corner and got hold of his throat. It must have been funny—like Weber and Fields. I was choking him with my hands and keeping Adolph off by kicking backward with my feet. I didn't know what Adolph might do if I let him in."

When Morris Kohn at last relaxed his hold, the broker was glad to draw a check for three hundred and eighty-five dollars. Then Morris stood guard over him while Adolph ran to the bank and got the money in spot cash. So much for that!

One Sunday afternoon in the period when he was struggling back to a small solvency, Adolph Zukor went out Cottage Grove Avenue to see Morris Kohn on business. Morris, the maid informed him, had gone driving with a niece who was visiting at the house. In the meantime, Adolph spied a scrub game of baseball in a vacant lot next door. He vaulted the fence, begged a job at second base, took off his coat, and plunged into the fray.

Presently, Morris came along with the second daughter of Herman Kaufmann—his brother-in-law and his partner in the adventure of the North Dakota homestead. Lottie Kaufmann had fulfilled that promise of beauty which was one consideration drawing her parents back to Chicago. Slender, dark-eyed, with an exquisite skin and a pleasant wit, she had suitors a-plenty. When first she set eyes on her future husband, he was fielding a grounder. Between innings, Morris introduced them. The incident made so little impression upon Adolph Zukor that he has forgotten it; and to Lottie Kaufmann he was just another man. But one evening in the same week, Adolph called on Morris Kohn with a business perplexity. The household was playing cards. They invited him to join; and Adolph Zukor left the table violently in love with Lottie Kaufmann.

It was a slow wooing, for Adolph Zukor had many rivals; and uneventful on the surface. Morris Kohn and Herman Kaufmann thought for a long time that Adolph frequented their houses just to play cards with them. The shrewd Mrs. Kaufmann first suspected his deeper intentions. He seemed at the moment the least promising of all Lottie's suitors—this boy protégé of her brother with his childish baseball and his embarrassing burden of debt. But Mrs. Kaufmann had not struggled through the hard years of her Dakota homestead without acquiring some insight into men. Under the quiet but pleasant surface of this comely, clean-chiselled boy, she perceived the fires of power. Subtly—as is the way of mothers—she became his advocate with her daughter. Somehow, the state of affairs dawned on the family.

Although she kept that to herself, the attractive Lottie was agreeing with her mother. Presently the whole interested group understood that Lottie and Adolph intended to get married when and if Adolph pulled even with the world and reached the position to support a wife. Morris Kohn, the most successful member of the family, had taken the affair in hand; and so he ruled.

By now, through piece-work and odd jobs, Adolph had paid all his debts except that to the bank; and business was picking up. With the backing and endorsement of Morris Kohn, he tried a new enterprise. It involved risk, but "Nothing venture nothing have" was almost the first motto he learned in English. Adolph moved his establishment to an upper story in State Street. On the ground floor was a silk shop. Zukor hired space before its front windows for a show case displaying an array of his own fur novelties. Chief of these was a double stone-martin scarf. It differed from the single scarf through which the Novelty Fur Company had made its initial success in that it had two heads: one over each shoulder. The fashion budded and blossomed, as that for the shoulder cape had budded and withered. In a month or so, Adolph Zukor found it necessary to enlarge his working quarters. Before the end of that season, he had discharged his debt to the bank, was running ahead of the world.

And so on January 10, 1897, Adolph and Lottie went to the Temple with the whole Kaufmann family, even to the remotest cousin; and Max Schosberg came from Peoria to stand up as best man.

In the month before the marriage, Morris Kohn revealed a plan which he had revolved for some time in his head. Manufacturing, he believed, was the profitable department of the fur business. He had long wanted to enter it, but he lacked experience. Adolph could bring that experience, and more. His circle recognized him as the cleverest young designer in Chicago. Therefore, Morris Kohn proposed a partnership—he to furnish most of the working capital and the judgment of raw furs, Adolph Zukor to supply the technique. Contemporaneously with the wedding, they formed the firm of Kohn & Company, manufacturing furriers.

The newly married couple established themselves in a flat on the West Side. Presently, things were going so well that without taking chances on the future they could employ a maid. It was only eight years since Adolph Zukor, his apprenticeship at Szalka expired, jingled in his pocket the first silver coins that he could ever call his own. At about the same period, Lottie Kaufmann was crawling back to Chicago from that sod house in Dakota. Such is the magic of America! The future seemed to stretch ahead gloriously secure. Some day, Adolph Zukor was going to be a big man in the fur business. Imagination leaped no higher than that.

Though once, imagination seemed for a moment to pierce the mists. It was four years since Adolph Zukor, visiting the World's Fair, breezed by that little side show which held the crude tachyscope moving picture of a walking elephant. Edison, as I have said, intended to exhibit his motion-picture machine at the Fair, but his mechanics and partners did not get the parts ready in time. In 1894, however, his company put out on the market his kinetoscope, a peep-show device. You dropped a coin into the tall box, applied your eye to the little black chute, and a picture which seemed about half as big as an average book page performed for nearly a minute. The subjects appealed not so much to the emotions of the beholder as to his sense of wonder at the marvels of science. Two girls—one of them afterward famous as Ruth St. Denis—did a life-like skirt dance. A pranksome boy shook pepper before a man at a desk; he sneezed in a life-like manner. By the end of that year, the original Edison Kinetoscope Parlours had opened: the first on Broadway, the second in Masonic Temple, Chicago, the third—Baccigalupi's—on Market Street, San Francisco.

Events began to move more swiftly. Two adventurous brothers named Latham saw the kinetoscope on Broadway; and, being sporting characters, conceived the idea of a moving-picture prize fight. They matched Mike Leonard and Jack Cushing, second-raters. It took. Thereupon they arranged the "great Corbett-Courtney fight," between the champion of the world and an obscure sparring partner. This went six one-minute rounds to a real knockout. As the kinetoscope showed it, the spectator dropped another nickel at the end of each round.

Going on, the Lathams conceived the idea of moving pictures on a screen instead of in a peep-hole; with the help of their father, Mayor Woodville Latham, they devised a crude projector to produce that result. And in April, 1895, they showed their pictures to the press of

New York. Thomas A. Edison, interviewed next day on the subject of this new sensation, called the Lathams infringers of his patents. As for projecting moving pictures onto a screen—he had done that himself. "But there's no commercial future in it," said Edison. Next month the Lathams opened on Broadway the first real screen show. The programme included Carmencita, the dancer, and a brief episode of a boy teasing a man on a park bench.

Little by little, such inventors as Armat, Woodville Latham, and Edison in America, Paul and Lumière in Europe, were improving that imperfect instrument, the projector. By 1896, Thomas A. Edison, persuaded tardily that the screen was the thing, had put out his new machine, the "vitascope"; and Lumière had devised for France a projection even better.

That same year, vaudeville saw the possibilities of the screen. In April, Koster and Bial's Music Hall at Herald Square, New York, ended its programmes with a vitascope show; the subjects included a fragment of Hoyt's farce, *A Milk-White Flag*, a pair of dancing girls, and the surf breaking against the chalk cliffs of Dover. It shared the honours of the theatrical week with Albert Chevalier, who made his first American appearance on the same programme. A little later, Vitascope added a street scene in Herald Square, *The Arrival of the Black Diamond Express*, and a parade of the New York mounted police. Lumière's cinematograph, which had similarly broken into vaudeville in London, presented as a further step a comic scene of a man watering with a hose in a garden, and a mischievous boy so managing things that the water squirted into the man's face. . . . For the collection and correlation of these facts, I am indebted—as every other historian of the screen must forever be—to Terry Ramsaye, moving-picture journalist. While the pioneers were still alive, he spent years of painstaking and expensive investigation in getting for his *Million and One Nights* the exact truth about these early, obscure beginnings.

Then the screen took a timid step toward drama. May Irwin had just made a great success with *The Widow Jones*. In this comedy, John C. Rice kissed her long and unctuously while his partner in bliss talked out of the corner of her generous mouth. All America was talking of the May Irwin Kiss. Vitascope purchased from Miss Irwin the right to immortalize this bit on the film, and put out the product over the Orpheum circuit. The early projectors were so made that any scene could be at once repeated. And audiences in the vaudeville houses used to encore The Kiss six or seven times.

Adolph Zukor remembers that in 1905 or thereabout he saw the signs of the old Edison kinetoscope in Masonic Temple, entered, invested a nickel in a view of the new wonder. But it produced so little impression that he does not now remember what he saw. Then, in the period when he and Lottie Kaufmann were awaiting

Mrs. Adolph Zukor

Marcus Loew

their wedding day, he took her to Hopkins Theatre. The show ended with the May Irwin Kiss. This perfect representation of human beings, bigger than life and moving as in life, lit a fire in his imagination. He was working mightily at that period. The next night he went back to the shop after dinner, intending to spend the whole evening over a design. But toward nine o'clock he closed up and went again to the theatre—drawn irresistibly by that fascinating marvel. There, however, it all ended for the time being. The seed so planted was to lie ungerminate for seven more years.

CHAPTER VIII

ZUKOR BECOMES A SHOWMAN

THE firm of Kohn & Company, manufacturing furriers, struggled through a first year of adjustment wherein profits were small and uncertain, and then went forward to a reasonably large success. By the end of the century, Morris Kohn had yielded to the importunities of his partner—"always in a hurry"—and opened a New York branch. Thenceforth, Morris lived a great deal on limited trains between New York and Chicago. Older and better skilled in English than Adolph Zukor, he played the part of "outside man." He saw customers, bargained for raw material, presided at the front of the shop. Zukor, with his talent for design, served mostly behind the scenes as superintendent of production.

The Eastern branch did well. And at about the turn of the century, the partners hatched an idea. New York was strengthening its position as fashion centre for the United States; the West merely confirmed styles which the metropolis had elected six months before. In Chicago one must needs gamble in his buying; guess a season ahead what material was going to be fashionable. In New York, on the contrary, one could get his orders with the first turn of the fashion and then buy his materials as needed. So Adolph Zukor moved to New York, and put their establishment in Twelfth Street near Broadway on a factory basis. Morris Kohn remained behind to close up the Chicago business, and then followed.

Zukor had by now two children: Eugene and Mildred. They found a comfortable flat at the corner of One Hundred and Eleventh Street and Seventh Avenue, a district which was then a German and Jewish quarter.

Marcus Loew lived on the opposite corner. To Zukor, he was then merely a passing business acquaintance; Morris Kohn knew him better. Loew, who began life as a newsboy on the East Side, had drifted like Zukor into the fur trade; had branched out as a salesman. Finally he set up for himself as a broker in raw furs. His sales route took him West, where he came into competition with Morris Kohn. These lively and able rivals first met in a St. Paul hotel.

"I was registering at seven o'clock in the morning," says Kohn, "when the clerk told me that another fur salesman, named Loew, had a room. I went up at once, for I wanted a look at him. He was packing to catch a train and—at that hour in the morning—he was wearing a top hat and a fur-lined coat. He must have noticed me staring at the hat, for he winked and said, 'I wear 'em to impress 'em.'"

Twice, on a bad turn of the fashion, Loew had gone down to the edge of bankruptcy. Now he was climbing back again. Zukor and Kohn used habitually to meet him at the old Hotel St. Denis for a good luncheon and a good laugh—Loew was the wit of his circle. Also, from the windows of his apartment, Marcus Loew's little son Arthur used sometimes to wave at a baby in the Zukor window across the street. Coached by her mother, Mildred Zukor would wave back. . . . These were her first exchanges of courtesy with her future husband.

Then rose another of those crises which have spotted Adolph Zukor's fortunes. The plan for conquering New York was not new or original. Other firms waited for the verdict of fashion before beginning to buy raw stock, "as needed." Thereupon, owing to the demand, the price of the favourite fur would shoot upward until it afforded a narrow margin of profit or no profit at all. In New York, as in Chicago, one must guess at the trend six months ahead; must gamble. Adolph Zukor, feeling himself crowded again toward the wall, plunged into one of his spasms of hard, concentrated work. He used to bring raw furs home at night and stitch out designs until Mrs. Zukor drove him to bed.

Eugene Zukor's definite memories of childhood date from this time. "Our house always smelled of fur," he says. "And I used to wish that Dad would get into some other business. Even now, I'm physically uncomfortable in a fur shop!"

However, by work, economy, and shrewdness, Kohn & Company pulled without much loss through that first hard year. Next season, following the custom and necessity of their business, they gambled—on red fox. The wheel of fashion turned, and the little ball dropped into the pocket opposite their stake. Red fox became a sensation. By 1904, Kohn & Company, though not a big firm, enjoyed a reputation for soundness and stability. Especially it had an A-1 rating with the banks. Now, Adolph Zukor was worth between one and two hundred thousand dollars.

Enter then into his life a current which sprang from remote sources.

The populace of these United States had not found as yet any suitable and darling form of amusement. The ten- twenty- and thirty-cent shocker was repeating itself. In those days, Owen Davis used to write a new melodrama in two weeks; allowing for vacations and pauses to conduct rehearsals, he fathered twenty a year.

"How did you ever keep up such a pace?" a writing woman inquired of him years later.

"Why not? I had a good plot!" responded Davis.

Nervously the herd was flocking to new, glittering enterprises which attracted but failed to satisfy. Nervously, showmen and managers were reaching for the formula which ever eluded them. Fred Thompson and "Skip" Dundy, a mechanical genius and a shrewd business man, achieved a great success at the Buffalo World's Fair with their glorified scenic roller coaster, "A Trip to the Moon." They went on to build Luna

Park at Coney Island, New York: a demesne of amusement whose governing principle was mechanical fantasy. This gave impulse to the amusement parks which had already sprung up over the United States. These establishments, however, were a little expensive to the consumer. Ten cents for this and twenty-five for that mount up to quite a figure; especially when the spender is a working man taking his family for a day's outing.

There was another limitation. Terry Ramsaye says wisely, "The populace loves to believe." That was later to stand a governing principle of the moving-picture business; though few, even while applying it, understood the principle. And a voyage by roller coaster through the Caves of the Moon, with dwarfed inhabitants singing curious wailing music through the copper-red foliage, aroused the intellectual impulse of wonder but not the emotion of belief.

All this time the formula lay wrapped up and addressed at the very feet of the showmen and managers; but they never saw it. During the years when Kohn & Company struggled with ladies' fashions, the moving picture was coming slowly out of the little peep-boxes and on to the screen. "Store shows" began to appear in the poorer amusement quarters of our cities, offering moving pictures, often associated with the cheapest of cheap vaudeville. The pictures ran two "subjects" to a reel. (A modern-feature moving-picture show is six or seven reels long.) Small and ignorant people held the

business of exhibition. Most of the early contracts are
signed, on the part of the exhibitor, with crosses!

At about this period, a young bank clerk of St. Louis
named Frank Meyer acquired a taste for "the pictures"
and let his imagination play on their possibilities. Half-
disguised, he dodged through the slums and sidled in
at the ticket-taker's door, dreading lest some acquaintance see him and report his bad habit to the bank. After
he took the plunge and went into the business of motion-
picture distribution, the ladies of his banking circle
dropped him from their lists.

When these little picture houses began to attract
public attention, reformers and uplifters took frantic
alarm. Moving-picture technique was still so crude that
the audience, in order to see action on the screen, must
sit in total darkness. That gave opportunity for "spoon-
ing," the mild Victorian ancestor of our modern "pet-
ting"; therefore was it dangerous to the morals of the
populace. Europe had produced a few pictures with a
slant toward what the trade called afterward "that sex
stuff." The positives of these pictures have gone long
since to the scrapheap; and I have never found any old
witness of such iniquities. It is impossible, therefore, to
say whether in our own time even reformers would consider them so very vicious. Nor were they produced
widely. But that was enough for minds afflicted with
the common human infirmity, suspicion of a new thing.
Generally, the prosperous and respectable first heard

of the motion-picture craze through city ordinances for suppression or regulation of these "slum theatres."

As for production, that lay still in control not of artists or showmen, but of engineers and mechanics. For the business, in this early stage of the game, was the prey of odd circumstances. No one man invented the moving picture. Both the camera which records the fluttering image and the projector which throws it onto the screen were the compound of many devices. Edison, it is true, laid his finger on the weak point in the camera; probably to him belongs the major credit. However, he stopped far short of perfection. Some of the minor improvements were invented almost simultaneously by different men. As these inventions became important, there followed a complex, tiresome series of lawsuits over patents and prior rights. So it happened that all who dealt with the production of moving pictures had their minds fixed not upon the finished product, but upon the tool.

In effect, the companies which manufactured apparatus governed the business. After the formation of the Moving Picture Patents Company and the General Film Company—the so-called "film trust"—they governed it in fact. The men in charge were concerned mostly with selling or leasing their machines; not with catching the nickels at the box office. At first they created film stories only as a means of giving the machines something to do, thereby creating demand.

To-day, the radio is passing through somewhat the same period of development. And, being mechanics, they thought of art in mechanical terms. The first curiosity of the public had died away. People no longer came to the films just to satisfy their sense of wonder at seeing a photograph move. They wanted now something which stirred the mind or emotion, just as on the spoken stage. And generally these early producers tried to satisfy that desire by mechanical "stunts"—a city destroyed at the touch of a magician, or a realistic devil bursting out of a volcano. The startling mechanical effects of the screen, such as the fade-in, long preceded the real film story. Instead of working toward Ramsaye's vital principle, "The public likes to believe," these early producers were working away toward unreality.

Nevertheless, the narrative element began to worm its way in. But with less than five minutes to a story, these first film narratives were primitive and childish—the pranks of small boys, the lollygagging of comedy lovers, the escape of a bicycle thief. The imperfect machine still blurred slow motion with irritating flashes; rapid action suited it best. Hence rose the "chase pictures"; in half the films of that period, someone ran after someone else. And yet the people of our less affluent city districts paid in increasing numbers their nickels at the box office; restrained as it was by sheer human blindness to commercial possibilities, the film was going ahead.

Adolph Zukor saw no more than the rest. He went

constantly to drama and vaudeville; along with lawn tennis, which had succeeded baseball in his enthusiasms, the theatre was his favourite diversion. But he had never witnessed a moving picture except on a vaudeville bill. The seed planted by the May Irwin Kiss still lay dormant.

He was to edge toward the moving picture through a by-path. When in 1894 and 1895 Edison began general distribution of his peep-show-in-a-box, the "kinetoscope parlours" grew into "nickodeons." Against one wall of these brilliantly lighted establishments stood a row of moving-picture machines; against the other, phonographs with ear-pieces for the individual auditor. The phonograph did not become a universal household luxury until ten years later. All these machines operated on the slot principle; a five-cent piece was the master key. As time went on, the cost of machines and materials fell; newcomers, competing with established firms, found it possible to cut prices to one cent.

In Buffalo lived Mitchell Mark, sprung like most of the characters in this story from humble origins. He had served as agent for the Edison devices, and knew this business. Mark conceived a simple yet brilliant idea, which he put experimentally into practice. He added to moving-picture boxes and phonographs all the existing penny-in-the-slot amusement machines of the country fairs, such as registering punching-bags, automatic fortune-tellers, devices for testing strength. These he gathered up into one establishment which showed them at a standard price of one cent apiece; and he named it the Penny Arcade. It succeeded; evidently Buffalo liked the idea. Proceeding cautiously, he tried out the plan in One Hundred and Twenty-fifth Street, New York, and proved to himself that the appeal of the Penny Arcade was universal, not local. In 1903, Mark prepared seriously to invade the metropolis. However, he lacked at the moment either the funds or the inclination to invest much of his own money in the venture.

Now among the large and growing family connection of the American Zukors was one Max Goldstein. The clan describe him as "a young fellow with a lot of good schemes but no money to back them." One day toward the end of that year, he called at the offices of Kohn & Company in East Twelfth Street, and laid before Kohn and Zukor the glittering idea of the Penny Arcade. There were millions in it; he needed only the loan of three thousand dollars to buy a partnership.

Kohn and Zukor listened to him open-minded; found the idea promising. They lent him three thousand dollars; then, fired with his enthusiasm, themselves invested in the company. So, in the amusement season of 1903-1904, the Penny Arcade opened in South Union Square with five owners—Mark, his Buffalo partner Wagner, Max Goldstein, Morris Kohn, and Adolph Zukor. It paid from the beginning. In the first year the slots swallowed up one hundred and one thousand dollars in

pennies; and notwithstanding the heavy overhead incident to starting such an enterprise, the Penny Arcade
returned twenty per cent. net profit on the investment.
They had, it seemed to them, the long-sought showman's formula for getting all the people all the time.

Now, a quarter of a century afterward, both Kohn
and Zukor laugh when they remember how the Penny
Arcade, a small flier in comparison with their established
fur business, absorbed from the first their attention and
interest. It was the blood working in them. "Every
Hungarian is either a peasant or an artist; often both."
And every Hungarian, be his origin Magyar or Semitic,
has something of the showman. All through Europe,
Hungarians sprinkle the theatrical and amusement business; in some countries they dominate it. Kiralfy, our
first imaginative showman, belonged to that breed.
Kohn and Zukor were drifting toward the vocation for
which they were born.

But presently, the Penny Arcade generated an interest far less remote. If it paid so well in Fourteenth
Street, why not in Harlem, the Bowery, Second Avenue,
Eighth Avenue, all quarters where simple people hun-
gered for cheap amusement? And beyond that lay a
thousand American cities, each an unworked gold mine.
They formed a kind of subsidiary company to exploit
the idea in other Eastern cities. And now, Marcus Loew
enters the show business. He had of late struck up an
acquaintance with David Warfield, come under fascina-

tion of the footlights. When Kohn, Zukor, and Mark opened the Penny Arcade he begged for a chance to buy a share. That company was full, but they let him into the subsidiary—for a few thousand dollars which grew to twenty-five millions.

Small though the return was for the moment, Kohn felt justified in giving the Penny Arcade his whole attention while Zukor ran the fur business. Within a month, obscure trouble had arisen. Not only was the arcade over-owned, but three of the owners—Zukor, Mark, and Kohn—were big and positive characters; in the course of the next fifteen years they all battered their way to wealth. The partners differed on policy; their irritation burst into a fight for control. Nevertheless, before the year ended the Penny Arcade had established in uptown New York, in Philadelphia, and in Boston a litter of offspring. Some of the partners wanted now to expand even faster in order that they might solidify their position before competitors appeared. Some were for holding back until they had more capital and experience.

Adolph Zukor, conducting the fur business in Twelfth Street while his mind dwelt elsewhere, belonged to the expansionist faction. He was still "in too much of a hurry." And there he sat with no hand in the actual management of the thing, learning even the details of the daily rumpus second-hand from Morris Kohn.

"Very well," said Morris Kohn one night, "you go

over and see if you can run the Penny Arcade, and I'll attend to the furs."

Adolph Zukor plunged into the new job, and found it from the first more difficult than he thought. But for all the irritation, he felt the glow of showmanship. By the end of two months he decided to abandon the fur business and throw his fortune with the Penny Arcade. He bought Morris Kohn's holdings. Then, having a good offer, they sold the fur house of Kohn & Company. Morris Kohn travelled West to close up the branch house.

When Kohn returned to New York, Adolph Zukor was practically beaten. The original Penny Arcade had taken in other partners. They had combined against him. He had reached an impasse.

"All right, Adolph," said Morris Kohn, "now I'm willing to have a try at it. Suppose you sell back your interest to me." Adolph accepted on the spot.

This was in 1905, the year when Adolph Zukor turned thirty-two. For the first time in his life, he was downed, really downed—a defeat spiritual, however, rather than material. He had lost little or no money in the affair of the Penny Arcade. He found himself with a fluid working capital of nearly two hundred thousand dollars, and for the present nothing to do with it. He began to look round for a good opening in the business of showmanship. For to that he found himself committed. He liked the game—its gaiety and glitter and movement, its sociability, and the sense of standing host to the world.

Let me finish here with some of the careers which flowed from troubled sources to pleasant lands through the channel of the Penny Arcade on Union Square. Mitchell Mark never again associated himself directly with his old partners. He "got into pictures" nevertheless. It was he who built later the Strand Theatre in Broadway, at the time the most important moving-picture palace in the world. Morris Kohn, after he took over Adolph Zukor's share in the Penny Arcade, formed the Automatic Vaudeville Company; the name explains its purpose. By negotiations whose details do not concern us, he acquired control and began to spot the community with penny arcades. At once, he drew Emil Shauer into the combination.

Here comes another of those alliances by matrimony —already so complex that I cannot blame the reader for growing confused. This one is a double link. Emil Shauer, born in America of a Bohemian couple, married Julia Kaufmann, sister-in-law to Adolph Zukor, and niece to Morris Kohn; she was born in that sod house of North Dakota. And Emil Shauer's sister had married Morris Kohn. Though not Hungarian, the Shauer family has a native taste for showmanship. Emil's brother, a chess player just below the championship class, served until his early death as the brains of the Automatic Turkish Chess Master in Chicago's Eden Musée. However, Shauer began life in a Chicago department store, and worked up to a buyer's job.

On his way to Europe, he visited his relatives in the Penny Arcade. The performance tickled his keen sense of humour. He agreed to help out by searching for novelties abroad. In Paris, he found an Automatic Gypsy Fortune-Teller which performed a realistic pantomime as it delivered the card. He bought the American rights for the Penny Arcade. On the voyage home, he amused himself by writing hopeful but cryptic prophecies for the fortune-cards; and all the automatic gypsy machines, even to this day, use those little jokes of Shauer's. When Kohn offered him a slice of the Automatic Vaudeville Company and a salary as manager, he threw up his good prospects in the dry-goods business to accept.

They both rose. Kohn's commercial sense and his talent for mechanics made him before long the eminent figure among exhibitors of penny arcades. Then the moving picture began slowly to out-distance all other devices for cheap amusement. Kohn saw that coming; and when about 1909 the stream of pennies dwindled, he slid painlessly over into motion-picture exhibition. Never again in the centre of Adolph Zukor's enterprises, he operated nevertheless on their outskirts. He has retired from business now—"with as much money as is good for me," he says. His country estate behind the western palisades of the Hudson lies near Adolph Zukor's; for after the temporary irritation raised by the mad situation in that original Penny Arcade, they settled down as affectionate kinsmen whose careers ran parallel. Emil Shauer, on the other hand, in time joined Adolph Zukor. His likeable personality, his sense of humour, and his experience with Europe played their part in developing the motion picture as a major American export.

A few weeks after Zukor left the Union Square Arcade, Loew found that his partners wanted to force him out of the subsidiary company. "All right, gentlemen," he said, "if we can't be happy together, let's be happy apart." And he sold out for the exact amount of his original investment. But he had found his beloved career; ladies' furs attracted him no longer. He stayed in the amusement business. . . . However, we are not quite finished with Marcus Loew.

The penny arcades, though they sickened in 1909, did not die. On the fringe of any amusement quarters in our greater cities you will find still these little tinsel establishments complete even to the peep-show motion pictures and the automatic gypsies. William Schork, the contemporary Penny Arcade king, began his rise as night watchman for that pioneer establishment in Union Square South. For him, too, it made magic!

CHAPTER IX

THE GREAT TRAIN ROBBERY

ℰNTER now, and by the side door, William A. Brady. Big, vital, cordial, witty, reckless, generous, one hundred per cent. masculine, he was born to bear a nickname; and his world still calls him "Billy Brady." He was the first of our eminent pugilistic managers and promotors; among other champions he handled James J. Corbett. In those days of saloon champions and mixed-ale preliminary fighters, pugilism had an aura of disreputability. Gradually, Brady edged over into the general amusement business, and after he married his leading woman, Grace George, he abandoned all connection with the prize ring. In 1905, he had out many ventures, ranging from Broadway productions to a baseball club.

In Chicago, Brady stopped one night before a cheap show whose front bore the electric legend, "Hale's Tours." Outside, a long queue of men, women, and children was waiting for the next exhibition to open. Such a phenomenon is fresh scent to a showman. Brady jostled his way in. He found himself occupying a perfect imitation of a railway carriage, which ended in an observation platform. When the seats were full and the door closed, the uniformed ticket-taker became the conductor.

"All aboard!" he called, and signalled to the imaginary engineer. Immediately the seats began swaying and rattling; a whistle blew in the distance; and the crunching of wheels sounded from below. As the train "started up," there began on a screen at the end of the observation platform a moving picture representing for one reel the ascent of Mont Blanc by scenic railway. Except for colouring, the illusion was perfect; you seemed indeed to be travelling on a rather unsmooth railway up the Alps.

When the conductor herded out the satisfied crowd, Brady stood on the sidewalk and watched through three performances. Business kept up all the evening. It looked like a gold mine, and Brady asked questions. This novelty, the doorkeeper informed him, came from Kansas City; Chief of Police Hale invented it and owned the patents. It had just reached Chicago; "territory" was still for sale. At once, Brady proceeded to Kansas City, dickered for a day with Chief Hale, and returned to New York owner of the Atlantic Coast rights.

At exactly the same period Adolph Zukor, having withdrawn from the Penny Arcade, found himself and his money out of employment. The theatrical world is given to gossip. Within a week, news of Brady's minor venture in amusement had spread abroad. So one afternoon Adolph Zukor, whom Brady knew casually as a small figure in the amusement world, called at the office.

"I have heard about Hale's Tours," he said, "and I want in."

Brady had several reasons for sitting down and talking it all over. He was struggling for a secure foothold as a theatrical manager. Already Broadway assumed that air of superiority toward the moving picture which held the film back from its destiny for so many years and closed the golden door of opportunity to so many managers. To appear as manager and sole owner of Hale's Tours might injure his standing. Here was a man willing to acknowledge ownership; and one with experience in small amusements. Further, Zukor proposed an ideal location—46 Union Square South, next door to the Penny Arcade. Past this row floated of evenings more people who would be likely to patronize a cheap show than past any other in New York. Finally, now that he saw for the first time into the mind of this casual acquaintance, Brady began to conceive for him an admiration which grew stronger with every passing year. "He didn't talk easily, but he always said something; and I could see that he had a lot of common sense." Before Zukor left the office, he had bought an equal partnership. Brady was to furnish experience and counsel; Zukor to manage the show.

Hastily they installed a "train" at 46 Union Square.

It was an immediate hit; during the first week the queue waiting for admission stretched halfway down the block. For once, Adolph Zukor had found a partner as much in a hurry as himself. The varnish was not dry on their apparatus in Union Square before they had opened another exhibition in Newark, had begun building in Boston and Pittsburgh.

The scheme involved a weekly change of programme; Chief Hale, in putting his invention on the market, had raked the world for views of famous scenery filmed from the rear of a moving train—such as the passes of the Rockies, the heights of the Andes, the palisades of the Hudson. The original show at 46 Union Square had changed its bill once or twice when receipts began mysteriously to dwindle. The same thing happened in Newark, Boston, and Pittsburgh—two or three weeks of full houses, and then a slump. Brady, the more experienced showman, put his finger on the weak point.

"It's a one-time show," he said. "I should have seen that! People are interested in the stunt, not the picture. Once they've had the experience, they won't come again. Better close it up and pocket our losses."

The typical Broadway showman puts out ten ventures at once, expecting to lose on nine of them and to recoup on the successful tenth. The experienced Brady was inured to that process; Zukor was not. He believed that Hale's Tours would yet pull through, and begged for a few weeks more. Those few weeks nearly ruined them, for attendance dwindled progressively.

Then, passing a little storehouse in Pittsburgh, Adolph Zukor saw a lurid poster advertising *The Great Train Robbery*. By way of keeping his eye on a rival, he paid his nickel, entered with the crowd. And for the second time in his life he found himself thrilled by a moving picture.

He was seeing, as a matter of fact, the contemporary climax of the art. A modern director, witnessing *The Great Train Robbery* in the National Board of Censorship's exhibit of antique films, laughs at its awkward technique. But it has merits which stand up still; and it compared to its predecessors as a well-rounded short story to a newspaper sketch. For one thing, it was the longest film ever produced in America. When Edwin S. Porter, its creator, announced his intention of making a picture which would run for a whole twelve minutes, the business called him insane. A few years later they said the same thing, and for a similar reason, of Adolph Zukor. . . .

Porter packed his twelve minutes with action. *The Great Train Robbery* told the story without the aid of captions; nor would captions have added anything. You see the bandits riding on their raid; you see the station agent working in his office. The bandits raid the agent, flash on his telegraph key the signal which halts the train at the siding. They hold up the train crew, blow the express safe, kill the messenger, force the passengers to stand in line, rob them. Meanwhile, the agent's little daughter, bringing supper in a dinner pail, discovers the crime. She cuts her father loose. He notifies the sheriff. There follows the "pursuit scene" grown since so conventional. Finally the posse surrounds the bandits, who fight to the death behind fallen horses. When the last man has rolled over dead, the film seems logically finished. But no—onto the screen springs a close-up of the Bandit Chief, masked and menacing. He draws his revolver and discharges all its chambers at the audience.

I saw *The Great Train Robbery* during its first run in vaudeville, and it appealed mightily to the little boy in me, so that I have remembered it all these years. Last year I saw it again, and it still had a thrill—especially that final scene, which to-day any jury of censors would condemn without leaving their seats.

Vaudeville was then the approved outlet for a new film. *The Great Train Robbery* had run on all the circuits to the great profit of its producer, and now, at reduced prices, was being peddled among the little five-cent store shows in the humbler tenderloins of our big cities. Watching it through two performances, Adolph Zukor hatched an idea.

Terry Ramsaye, who has observed his peculiarities for many years, has noted that when Zukor thinks things out, he works off his superfluous energies by walking. That night, he walked Pittsburgh into the small hours. Next morning, on his own responsibility, he rented a set of Porter's films. Thereafter, as soon as the "train" reached the summit of Mont Blanc or the head of the Royal Gorge, the jiggling machinery stopped and *The Great Train Robbery* began on the screen. Interviewing his customers at the door, Zukor found that they liked this piece of melodrama better than the scenic tour. Business began to pick up.

But too late, Brady felt. Preparing for a busy season on his own account, much more interested in his Broadway productions than in any flier with a five-cent show, he took time to run over the statements of Hale's Tours, and fell into profound pessimism. They had sunk a small fortune in the machinery of the enterprise; each car, with the apparatus which made it sway and clatter, cost from six thousand dollars to eight thousand dollars. And it was mere scenery; only scrap iron and kindling once the show closed. They had liabilities of one hundred and eighty thousand dollars; and assets, mostly frozen, of little more than one hundred thousand. Though *The Great Train Robbery* had stimulated receipts, the company was still running behind.

"In this business," he told Zukor, "you must know when you're beaten. A thing goes or it doesn't go. Many a manager has ruined himself by hanging to a losing proposition. *Great Train Robbery* and all, it's still a one-time show."

Entrance to Hale's Tours, operated by Adolph Zukor in company with William A. Brady

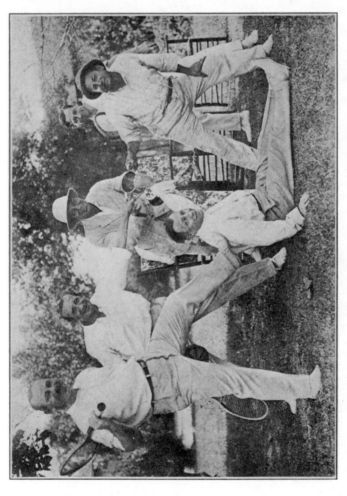

An interesting tennis group. Left to right—the late Marcus Loew, Sam Bernard, Milton Wolff, Lou Teller, and Lew Fields. Adolph Zukor is seated on the ground

"But how can we quit?" asked Zukor.

"Throw her into bankruptcy," said Brady. "That's fair and usual. This is a limited liability company. We wipe out our debts and lose only the few thousand we invested in the beginning."

To this day, Billy Brady remembers the effect of this proposal on his young and obscure partner.

"It was as though I'd touched him with a live wire," he says. "He bounced up from his chair and came at me with his hands out. I never dreamed he had such a temper. And he yelled, 'I won't go into bankruptcy! I won't!'"

When the partners recovered their balance, Adolph Zukor proposed a plan to regain solvency. He had been listening to the gossip of the little, submerged moving-picture world. Porter's masterpiece had started a slow movement forward. Although a twelve-minute film with a dozen actors, a mob, and trained horses seemed too daring an enterprise for general adoption, directors were beginning to introduce coherent stories; month by month their product improved. It was possible to get a reasonably steady supply of films which, though stopping far from ideal, drew the public. Zukor proposed frankly to scrap the machinery of Hale's Tours, to turn the houses into five-cent moving-picture theatres. On those terms, he believed, the company could return profits and eventually pay off its debts. At any rate, he wanted to make the try. Even yet, he failed in thorough mastery of the English language. Perhaps that defect served him in this argument so vital to his future career. An inarticulate man, struggling for expression while he talks common sense, achieves an impression of sincerity which no glib man can imitate.

"All right," said Brady at length, "go ahead and have your try. But don't get us further into the hole, and don't bother me with details."

Silently, persistently—as was his way—Adolph Zukor went to work. He made Brady's office his uptown head-quarters. Busy with a hundred other things, Brady paid this small, unsuccessful venture very little attention, except to satisfy himself that it was not losing any more money. At the end of two years, Adolph Zukor entered his office and laid a balance sheet on the desk. Brady ran through the papers, and whistled. The transformed Hale's Tours had begun to return a profit in its first year; now, at the beginning of the third, it had paid off the whole debt; and in the bank lay a small but encouraging dividend!

That, however, is going a little ahead of the story.

CHAPTER X

THE COMEDY THEATRE

*W*HEN Adolph Zukor persuaded his partner to salvage rhe Hale's Tours Company by means of the moving picture, he proceeded in a manner which perturbed the temperamental Brady. At the approach of summer he tightened up the shaky machinery of the doubtful enterprise, left it in competent hands, and took his family abroad for a leisurely tour of Europe.

"I was irritated at the time," said Brady twenty years later. "If I hadn't been so busy, and if it hadn't seemed such a trifling little side show to my Broadway enterprises, I think I'd have closed it all up then and there."

As for Zukor, he says merely: "I wanted to get away and think."

Also he was very, very tired. In 1894, as I have told before, he and Max Schosberg, flush with the first golden running of the Novelty Fur Company, had taken a boyish look at Europe. More than eleven years had passed since then, during which Adolph Zukor never knew a real vacation. Meantime, he had lived through spasm after spasm of anxious, concentrated, gruelling work—his struggle to get back on his feet after the collapse of the fur cape, his efforts to establish Kohn & Company in New York, his losing fight for control of the Penny Arcade, his scrambling and juggling to keep Hale's Tour Company out of bankruptcy. He had become conscious of an itching irritation over all his skin; in him the first signal—as specialists were afterward to inform him—of nervous exhaustion. Now, he had altered again the whole direction and purpose of his life. He was about to enter his third apprenticeship, though he realized that only dimly. He did realize that he faced another struggle, and needed all his strength.

"The most sensible thing he ever did," says Brady now.

He lingered awhile in Paris and Vienna, and then revisited Ricse. In the decade since he saw it last, more and more boys of the town had felt the stirring of ambition and emigrated to America. As a proof of prosperity, they were sending back remittances from their wages. But after all, these were only workmen or, at most, floorwalkers and clerks. Here came a native who seemed to Ricse a wealthy man. He had been partner in a New York fur busines; he was now a "theatrical manager"—little, orphan Adolph! Somewhat to his embarrassment—he having a sense of proportion—the Mayor turned out the Town Council to receive him. Evading further honours, he passed on to Berlin for a visit with Rabbi Arthur Liebermann, already established as the most eloquent of the younger Hebrew preachers in the German metropolis. Another leisurely look at Paris, and with the first touch of autumn he returned to New York entirely refreshed.

That is the surface of the matter. But underneath, in the depths of his wide-thinking, in-taking mind, Zukor had worked out his problem and mapped his future. The moving picture might have infinite possibilities. Though its mechanical devices and methods were still crude, they were improving constantly. He had seen a great advance, even in his own brief experience. Artistic improvement seemed just as inevitable. Some day—and perhaps soon—production would work its way out of the hands of mechanics and into that of showmen. Then—well, *The Great Train Robbery* proved how audiences would respond. In that day the moving picture might displace the spoken theatre. On paper, it was a simple problem in arithmetic. The "legitimate" stage charged a dollar and a half for an orchestra seat; it could not charge much less and continue to exist. The moving-picture house charged five cents, or at the most, ten. . . . He sailed for Europe in a state of uncertainty over his future. Hitherto, he had been merely an opportunist. While his natural bent had something to do with turning him from a fur manufacturer into a showman, accident had made him a specialist in motion pictures. From now on, however, the way lay clear and marked before him. He intended to play this one card, and to gamble on it everything he had. Also, it would seem, there rewoke in him a quality which he had shown in his youth, but which seems to have lain dormant during his early struggles with business—his faculty for thinking ahead. To that turn of mind—which became in later years a habit—many of his old associates attribute his later phenomenal success. The rest envisaged only to-morrow; Zukor's imagination was constantly analyzing and synthesizing a situation two or three years in the future.

He had named that little revamped store at 46 Union Square, South, the Comedy Theatre. There he settled himself in a cubby-hole over the auditorium and swung into another spasm of hard, concentrated work. Now that Zukor had buckled down, Brady paid little attention to this trifling side enterprise. Not once a month did he think to inquire how or what it was doing. Zukor, however, had all his eggs in the one basket. He was trying to squeeze every nickel he could out of the Comedy, whose tinny piano clanged day and night below him, and out of three smaller and more perplexing houses in Newark, Boston, and Pittsburgh. The Comedy, what with permanent seats and a passable stage, gave a reasonably good imitation of a regular theatre. The others still looked what they were—vacant stores in which the revampers had thrown up stages that seemed made of cardboard. The audiences sat on kitchen chairs, on benches, on the second-hand leavings of undertakers' parlours.

Marcus Loew, like Zukor forced out of the original Penny Arcade at Number 48, had himself embarked in the business of exhibiting motion pictures. Within the year, he was juggling finances for a string of five-cent motion-picture-and-vaudeville houses, mostly in Greater New York; in so far as anyone considered this humble business at all, he was a more considerable factor than his old friend of the fur trade. Their theatres stood in different parts of the city, they did not come into direct competition; and so they found themselves making common cause, working out a policy.

As yet the pictures were so crude, so uneven in merit, that a manager even of a five-cent house could not depend upon them alone. Fortunately for the infant industry, the vaudeville craze was on. Out of the East Side had emerged such popular figures as Weber and Fields, Dave Warfield, Francis Wilson. Every boy with a jig in his legs, every girl with a tune in her throat, nursed an ambition for the footlights. Promising semi-amateur material came cheap. You could get a passable songster, black-face comedian, or dance artist for twenty-five dollars a week; a team for forty dollars. Indeed, Loew considered himself more a vaudeville manager than a motion-picture exhibitor. At his first houses, the cinema merely filled in, cheaply, the space between the turns.

To Zukor, on the other hand, the vaudeville acts were an expensive necessity—a stabilizer of the show until such time as the pictures came into their own. Under patronage of these two men, and of the other unpretentious exhibitors whose houses were springing up all over the city, there arose a circuit of small-time vaudeville people, just graduated from the amateur class, who played all year round in New York and environs. Through this side door, Sophie Tucker, Eddie Cantor, and Lowell Sherman entered on their careers.

The Comedy occupied a fortunate site, perhaps the best for the purpose in New York City. It prospered from the first. Newark and Boston did passably. Pittsburgh, twelve hours away by train, was a perplexity. Zukor found difficulty in getting competent sub-management for a concern so small and cheap. It lost money steadily. Then came a depression in the steel business, forerunner to the brief but acute hard times which struck the country in 1907. Further, the city began to instal a tramway station in the same block, rendering the site, for the time being, most undesirable. Zukor found himself juggling his payroll on Saturday nights; again he faced the imminent prospect of bankruptcy.

When every month or so Brady asked carelessly, "How are the pictures going, Adolph?" Zukor replied with affected nonchalance:

"Oh, fine, Billy!"

As a matter of fact, he had thrown some of his own reserve funds into the venture; and Pittsburgh swal-

lowed them up. At no other time in a life full of crises
like this had Zukor worried so much.

Husband-like, while presenting a brave face to the
world he unbosomed himself at home. So one day, returning from the office, he found a moving van at the
door of his apartment house. Mrs. Zukor met him on
the stairs.

"I knew you'd never ask this, Adolph," said she,
"but we're moving to a small flat in One Hundred and
Forty-seventh Street. And I've discharged the maid."

They settled down to live small again, as they had
done in the early, struggling days after their marriage.
Mildred Zukor, destined to be heiress of two great fortunes, began at about this period to register her first
conscious memories. And she tells how the only family
diversion was a taxicab ride through the Park on Sunday
afternoons. Adolph Zukor used to walk whenever he
could, in order to save carfare. Then he found a purchaser for the troublesome branch of his business: a
Pittsburgh man, who had a faith equal to his own in the
future of motion pictures. Compared to the sum which
he and Brady had sunk in the equipment for Hale's
Tours and in the subsequent losses of this house, the
price was trifling. But it was better than nothing. Zukor
applied this access of funds to easement of the situation
in his New York, Boston, and Newark houses; drove
ahead.

Now, at last, the anticipated began to happen. The

pictures, though still very crude, were improving. The public was becoming "educated" to the screen. The newspapers had begun to notice the "moving-picture craze." In steadily increasing returns the business felt the run of the tide. Boston and Newark passed decisively and permanently into black figures. The Comedy Theatre was turning custom away. A year after he sold the Pittsburgh house came the day when Adolph Zukor arrayed himself in his nattiest garments, strolled casually into Billy Brady's office, and, with pardonable pride veiled by a nonchalant manner, laid on the desk a dividend check. All its debts paid, the old Hale's Tours Company was returning a profit of ten per cent!

Meantime, a new human factor had come into the business. In 1903, Herman Kaufmann, Mrs. Zukor's father—that merry and loyal soul who went pioneering with Morris Kohn in South Dakota—died suddenly in Chicago. Morris Kohn, let me recall to the reader, is Mrs. Kaufmann's brother; and Adolph Zukor is her son-in-law. Both have almost a mania for taking care of their relatives. In 1904, the year when they opened the Penny Arcade, they brought on the widow from Chicago, established her, with Frances the baby and Al Kaufmann her seventeen-year-old son, in a Harlem flat.

Al Kaufmann, born in that North Dakota sod house, seemed to have absorbed the free and sociable spirit of the old West. When the family moved back to Chi-

cago, he and his sister Julia (Mrs. Emil Shauer) entered together a public school on the South Side. His
high animal spirits, his joy in battle, and his pranks
made him so much trouble that Julia, with a little girl's
sense of propriety, used to say to her schoolmates, "He
isn't my brother; he's only a bad little boy of the same
name."

By the time he moved to New York he could whip any
boy of his size in the district. And New York went at
once to his head. "He bought him a cane and a pearl-
gray hat," says Mrs. Kaufmann, "and began to think
he owned Broadway." When the Penny Arcade opened,
Kohn and Zukor found him a place as ticket taker. He
began coming home late; much later, his watchful
mother found, than the closing of the Penny Arcade
justified.

In the small hours of a certain winter morning she
arose, travelled downtown by subway, and approached
the Penny Arcade. It was closed, but the front door
stood unlocked. Also, a dim light burned in the shooting-
gallery at the rear. There Mrs. Kaufmann came upon
her son, shooting craps on the floor. His companions—
caps, loud cravats, sweaters decorated with diamond
pins—the experienced Mrs. Kaufmann read the signs
at once. This costume, as well as their hard young faces,
betrayed them for East-Side gangsters. Family tradition
holds that one of them was Lefty Louie, afterward
executed for his share in the Rosenthal murder. When

she invaded the room, they sprang to their feet and hands went to hips, for they thought that it was the police. Before she finished with them, they wished it had been the police.

Mrs. Kaufmann took her son from the place, bore him home. Next day, a council of his mature relatives put down on him the screws of old-fashioned Jewish family discipline. They ruled that he couldn't be trusted in a tough district. He must keep away from the Penny Arcade. Morris Kohn got him a job at ten dollars a week in the basement of a lace house, and Mrs. Kaufmann confiscated his latchkey. For nearly three years he served like a convict, nailing boxes in that basement; and, spite of false promises, he still made only ten dollars a week. So he came to Adolph Zukor, pleading for parole. On his promise of strict virtue and propriety, Zukor employed him as house manager, ticket taker, general factotum.

He was a furious, instantaneous hit. Within six months he had become perhaps the most popular character in the district; known by his first name to every policeman, bartender, gangster, and ward politician. He arrived just in time. South Union Square and the abutting stretch of East Fourteenth Street were rising to the hectic climax of their impermanent little day as a cheap tenderloin. Tom Sharkey's saloon and dance hall, a block to the east, was drawing the sailor custom from the old Bowery. In its lee upsprung a dozen resorts as scandalous to propriety as New York has known in the past quarter-century. It seemed for a time a larger, cleaner, and less picturesque Barbary Coast.

However, one element which old San Francisco never knew troubled all the resorts and amusements of this district, from the lowest dive to the "first-class family resorts" like the Comedy and Penny Arcade. The East Side gangsters had begun to make Third Avenue and Fourteenth Street their headquarters. Except when important business of loft robbing or shooting took him abroad, Lefty Louie could always be found of nights in this region; likewise his companion of the Rosenthal murder and the electric chair at Sing Sing, Gyp the Blood. Monk Eastman and Humpty Jackson, both fated to die by pistol bullets, ruled their underworld from saloons under the Elevated. Keeping order was becoming a problem. Tom Sharkey, by virtue of his ability and record, served efficiently as his own sergeant-at-arms. The lower resorts employed Bowery toughs, six feet four inches tall and half as broad, who hit first and reasoned afterward.

Al Kaufmann served not only as house manager but as bouncer for the Comedy Theatre. Though perfectly capable of taking care of himself in a fight, he never found it necessary to fight. He effected order through personality, tact, and subtlety. Knowing by face and name every gangster in the neighbourhood, he understood perfectly that they carried in their hip pockets

"Annie Oakleys" to all shows, dancing floors, and public exhibitions. When one of this element poked his cap and the turtle neck of his sweater into the ticket window, Al Kaufmann passed out a ticket and forgot the money.

Charlie Murphy himself, Grand Sachem of Tammany —it was his own district—noticed this lively boy with his talents as a mixer; marked him for promising human material. So through the lower fringes of Tammany ran the tacit order, "Keep off the Comedy." When, as happened once in a blue moon, Al Kaufmann was forced gently to eject a drunken sailor, half a dozen gangsters and Tammany stalwarts would rise up from the audience, sidle to the door, and volunteer their assistance. Adolph Zukor kept to his office on the floor above, or at most stood by the door at the period of the hourly emptying and questioned patrons as to what they most liked or disliked about the show. Before the year, indeed, everyone in Union Square thought that Al Kaufmann owned the place.

Al Kaufmann also extended his benevolent protectorate over that allied family institution, the Penny Arcade, next door. That, still the more considerable show of the two, swam now in prosperity. Expressing his mechanical bent, Morris Kohn invented a miniature electric railway which, running under the slot machines, touched a trigger in each and let a shower of pennies inundate the toy freight cars. This piece of showmanship, heavily advertised, drew great crowds to the Arcade at "collection hours"—five in the afternoon and nine at night. As the "moving-picture craze" increased, Kohn and Shauer leased the floor above and opened a five-cent cinema show. You mounted to it by an iridescent and illuminated glass staircase, under which ran a constant stream of water. In normal circumstances Zukor might justly have quarrelled with relatives who set up opposition next door, but at the moment he welcomed the move. Already the Comedy was packed at every performance; he was turning so many people away as to injure the reputation of his house for comfort and accessibility. Presently, the company into which he and Brady had faded Hale's Tours was returning dividends of twenty per cent.

What were the Comedy and the Penny Arcade giving the public by way of entertainment? Of late I have seen some of those old films. To draw a comparison with a thing infinitely more dignified, it is as though a habitual patron of the Globe Theatre, in the days when Shakespeare and Jonson wrote the play, Burbage and Kemp acted it, should have met by accident a team of mummers reciting a clownish dialogue at a country fair. Here were the roots from which grew the Globe, the Blackfriars, *Bartholomew Fair*, *Hamlet;* but to the eyes of a more sophisticated generation they were merely grotesques.

Taking conservatively a cue from *The Great Train*

Robbery, the mechanics and bankers who controlled moving-picture production were now making concessions to the human passion for a story. But a reel of a thousand feet remained their limit of length. That, indeed, was unusual; generally they put two stories onto one reel. The plots were so simple as to make a nursery yarn seem complicated and sophisticated. Ralph Kohn, son of Morris, used to play about the Penny Arcade. Unanimously, his elders have forgotten the simple narratives of these old films, but they stick in Ralph's head like his nursery rhymes.

"There was the masher film, for example," he says. "I'll bet it showed up in one form or another twenty times a year. A comedy character makes up to a lady on a park bench. Sometimes she's his wife in disguise. Sometimes she's just any girl. Anyhow, she calls a cop and there's a chase. Finally they catch him and the cop beans him. That's all! The Wild West stuff came just as often. The bandits rob a train or a bank or a stage or a grocery. The sheriff chases them and they die with their boots on."

Nine films out of ten were "comics" or brief melodramas. The tenth offered a love story built on that formula as old as human language: "Two lovers—love—the obstacle—the obstacle overcome." These ran, usually, two to the reel, giving the narrator about seven minutes with his audience.

Photography was still very uncertain; directors, usu-

ally the failures of "still" photographic studios, understood lighting only dimly. Irritating glimmers and jerky
action still blurred the images on the screen. No one as
yet understood moving-picture make-up; faces appeared
sudden black or ghastly white. The actors were the
small people of the legitimate stage. Established actors,
even when they needed the money, fought shy of the
cinema. To appear in a "film show" was to confess
cheapness; it prejudiced one's chances for a real job.
No one had learned as yet that the screen is a more
realistic medium than the stage; that even the best stage
acting seems affected before the camera. *The Great Train
Robbery* had told its story without titles; it remains in
that respect an archaic technical marvel. The lesser
directors had invented the title to supplement their
sluggish imaginations and to compensate for the very
brief time allowed them on the screen. To-day these
also seem strange and awkward. "John Tells Mary His
Love," read the legend, or, "Two Years Later, Bill the
Bandit Rode into Tucson"; and immediately you saw
John or Bill doing it. Though Porter and the forgotten
director of the May Irwin Kiss had introduced the
close-up, producers used the device but seldom; and
never, as nowadays, by way of registering the emotion
of a character. For it tended to expose the uncertainties
and defects of their photography and lighting. Said
Zukor in summing it all up years later: "They put
some brains into their mechanical devices and into

their sales department, but never by any chance into their films."

With his order of "finished" film—purchased by the foot—the exhibitor must take also the appropriate "paper." Early in the game, the producing companies had found a cheaper way than employing their own draftsmen, patronizing their own lithographers. The ten-twent'-thirt' road show was still the theatrical staple of the small towns. Hundreds of melodramas toured out of New York every year; of which a constant proportion went on the road. In such emergency, they had no use for the rest of their posters. The motion-picture producers bought up this stuff at waste-paper prices. Choosing a three-sheet which bore some remote resemblance to the subject of his current film, they sent it forth to the exhibitor. Sometimes the resemblance was remote indeed. "A Trip Through Hell!" announced one sensational poster; and the picture showed all the horrors of Dante's Inferno. The film, a half a reel long, was simply a trick Italian picture of a stage devil rising from the crater of Vesuvius. Indeed, the poster, not the film, seemed to govern the business. Sometimes when Al Kaufmann made his trial run of the newest programme, he discovered that he was repeating a film which he had exhibited two or three months before, only with a new poster!

When this happened, or when the current picture was especially dull or confused, Adolph Zukor juggled round his vaudeville talent to present some especially popular feature. The "song slide," achieving popularity at about this period, helped mightily. A robust tenor or a tinny soprano stood at one side of the proscenium arch rendering "She Was Bred in Old Kentucky," "In the Shade of the Old Apple Tree," or any other sugary love-song of the day, while the projector flashed on the screen coloured "still" photographs of the maiden and her lover. Now and then, on the other hand, came a film with a real laugh in it, a good story simply told, or a genuinely effective piece of romance. Always Zukor stood at the door as his audiences emerged, picking up friendly conversation about the show. Usually, he found his simple guests liked best the vaudeville turns. But when he presented one of these superior films they talked invariably not of the vaudeville actor but of the "pichur." More and more, Adolph Zukor's experience confirmed his original judgment. There was a great future in the business; but expansion must wait until producers realized the possibilities of their medium and gave the public something better—until "they put brains into the films."

· CHAPTER XI

THE TRUST GOES TO SEED

*A*DOLPH ZUKOR, inhibiting as best he might his native impatience, waited for seven long years.

To make comprehensible what follows, I must review briefly the curious state of the whole moving-picture business between 1905 when Zukor and Brady turned their Hale's Tour houses into "store shows," and 1912 when Zukor, defying the world, took matters dramatically into his own hands. I shall not trouble the reader with much chronology or with the details of tangled lawsuits and countersuits to which such careful historians as Ramsaye have devoted whole volumes.

I have called the first period of the American moving picture the age of the mechanic. Owners of the governing patents, or aspirants to such ownership, controlled the business. Concerned mainly with establishing their rights and selling or leasing apparatus, they produced films only by way of giving their machines something to do. And in the spirit of mechanics did they deal with artistic material. The second era, heralded by *The Great Train Robbery*, began just before Adolph Zukor entered the business. Even the mechanics now perceived that the public regarded the screen, not so much a vehicle for conveying the news or improving the mind with views of foreign lands, as a medium for telling a story.

Then came the series of events which in 1908 led the owners of the "Edison Patents" and the "Biograph Patents" to amalgamate as the Motion-Picture Patents Company. Its critics called this "The Film Trust." Whether or not it was a trust in the legal sense of the word, I am not competent to say. But the epithet passed into the argot of the film, and for convenience I shall use it. Perhaps the Trust might be a force yet, not a memory, had it contented itself with making and dispensing machinery and apparatus. However, the firms from which the Patents Company formed itself had already mixed inextricably the manufacture of apparatus and the production of pictures. The Trust, on behalf of nine or ten companies holding its license, sought absolutely to control production. In theory, none could use a motion-picture camera, none could distribute the finished film, without a licence—costing a half a cent a foot—from Motion-Picture Patents Company. All other picture makers were "outlaws."

Now here was a new mode of expression, a new medium for conveying thought. And it was as though when Gutenberg invented printing he had patented his process and thenceforth confined the subject matter of the press to writings by his office staff. The film was making its way—increasing in public esteem, whipping up public curiosity. Others, outside of the companies gathered under the Trust, wanted an opportunity to express themselves. A good many tried. As things stood they had perhaps the moral right; but the Trust had the legal right. Producing independent film was by way of breaking the law. Consequently and naturally, many of the early free lances were a trifle careless of all moral considerations. Those obscene films, bootlegged through the tenement quarters, which evoked the first municipal laws for regulation of moving-picture exhibition, came largely from independent producers of this class.

They violated not only morals but propriety and taste. One of them filmed the hanging of a negro in a Southern jail, omitting no ghastly detail. For years this piece of tainted celluloid dodged through the country just ahead of the sheriff and the police. Another showed a lynching; the actor, strung up by a trick rope, made realistic gestures with his pinioned hands and feet. Already children were knocking in clamorous flocks at the doors of the motion-picture theatres. To prosper—the Trust perceived—pictures must be "pure." By way of advertising their own purity and guarding themselves against crusaders, the licensed producers formed in 1909 the first voluntary censorship, whose successor is going yet. In their fight against the independents they needed favourable public opinion. "We produce only clean films" —this was their main argument with suspicious municipal authorities, newspapers, women's clubs.

To close an unlicensed film or to squelch an unlicensed

producer, the Trust—speaking generally—had only to bring an injunction. But this is a big country, full of hiding places; and moving-picture apparatus is compact and portable. The "independents," the "film pirates," worked unmolested in remote corners of the desert or the mountains and "free-lance" exhibitors showed their product in revamped stores through the small cities and towns. To uncover one quarter of these infringements, the Trust would have needed a force as big as the Prohibition Unit.

Faced with wrongs for which the law had no practical or effective remedy, the Trust itself stepped a little outside of the law. There followed years of melodrama as exciting as anything that the directors were putting on the screen. Free-lance producers, setting up their apparatus at some secret location, would be raided by gangs of young men who wore cauliflower ears. A brief free fight—and the raiders would depart with such of the apparatus as survived the affray. The independent producer had no legal remedy; he could not come into court with clean hands. "Western outfits," preparing to shoot a scene in Arizona or New Mexico, would find themselves mysteriously under fire. Some artist with the rifle was shooting from the bushes; not at them, but all around them. Kept up long enough, these tactics would cause the sudden resignation of actors and actresses uninured to the Wild West. Spies and private detectives dogged not only the leading independents but the officers and stars of the Trust. For the opposition was using its own rough tactics. Sometimes a new negative of a Trust firm came from the film bath rotting and ruined by the addition of some insidious chemical; and simultaneously a photographic expert, newly hired a few days before, would disappear without collecting his pay.

Eventually, the fight came out into the open. Both sides appealed to the public. The Trust emphasized its legal right and the moral purity of its product. The independents played on the "trust-busting" spirit of the time. The first modest moving-picture journals had their inception in the militant necessities of this fight.

While the bankers and mechanics at the head of the Trust struggled to maintain their monopoly of film production, they did not neglect their opportunity for monopoly of distribution. At first, they proceeded on the "states' rights" plan. To some local entrepreneur the producer sold the exclusive franchise to peddle its films in New York or Louisiana or California. The purchaser let out the subsidiary rights to exhibitors, and pocketed his gains or his losses. All these states' rights buyers were supposed to handle Trust films exclusively. Often, they tried to supplement their incomes by surreptitious addition of outlaw films. When the Trust discovered them at it there followed legal actions, withdrawals of patronage, even dramatic raids,

In 1909, it organized its exchangemen for continuous and regular distribution. But important men kept out from under its tent. Then in 1910 it formed the General Film Company, virtually a subsidiary, and started to buy up exchanges. A year or two more, and the agencies of the General Film Company covered the entire country, with the important exception of New York. There William Fox, afterward a large factor in film production, had enough capital and political backing to hold out. Now the Trust, which did business with no house that ever exhibited an independent film, could begin regular distribution of two new films a week. Outside of New York and one or two unimportant localities, the independents had to use the old states' rights plan. Zukor took his supply at first from the Trust; but shortly after the General Film Company was formed, he aligned himself with the independents.

The Trust had therefore some competition, which, under ordinary circumstances, might have developed the moving picture into its modern form. However, the circumstances were not ordinary. These competitors were merely sniping around the edges. All of them knew that any exceptionally fine and popular film, any startling new departure, would cause the Trust to draw its concealed weapon—the law of the land. As for the "regular" firms, they started bravely forward about 1907 or 1908; a few men of artistic impulse and background, like J. Stuart Blackton, began to produce one-reelers which really told a story in interesting form. Then about 1909 or 1910 they stopped and set.

The trouble was too much prosperity.

In 1908, there came to the Biograph as actor and director one David Wark Griffith. All through a roving and unsettled youth, life had been training him for this very job. As a newspaper reporter in Alabama and in Louisiana he had acquired a journalistic sense of the popular mind. He took to writing plays, thereby educating himself in dramatic form. His masterpiece was accepted by a Broadway manager and then, by a cruel whimsey of the theatrical business, sent to the storehouse. "And I lost twenty pounds just cursing fate," he says. Nature gave him expressive and mobile features and in the course of his adventures with rejected plays he learned that he could act. Needing money, he began playing small parts as a stop-gag. He found himself "resting," with hunger just round the corner. "And so," he says, "I sold myself down the river." He entered a studio as scenario writer at $10 a script and actor at $5 a day. This, he felt, spelt ruin to his stage career; but he had to eat.

The legitimate theatre of Broadway was still pulling its hobble skirts away from its hoydenish little cousin of Union Square. Any actor whose face appeared on the screen acknowledged himself to the profession as a cheap failure. When the Biograph Company, liking

Griffith's scenarios, offered him a job as director, the management had almost to sandbag him into acceptance. The certainty of fifty steady dollars a week probably turned the scale.

For years, indeed, he quarrelled with his fate, swearing, at the expiration of each contract, that he was going to quit the game, then reluctantly signing again. Griffith put new life not only into the Biograph but into the whole business. He began using the close-up to emphasize poignantly emotional moments. He invented "parallel action." He groped away from stage-acting toward the more realistic acting which suits the film. Above all, he was by training both a journalist and a dramatist; he knew how to tell a story. Other human discoveries of other companies were making their own improvements. They and Griffith borrowed each other's ideas back and forth. Yet perhaps he was the leading artistic spirit in that false dawn of the moving picture. Also, he found Mary Pickford.

This most famous of American women has stood subject for a dozen biographies. Here, I merely summarize her life. She was born Gladys Smith of Toronto, Canada; her father was of English extraction, her mother Irish. When she was five years old, her father—a purser on a transatlantic steamer—died suddenly, leaving his widow and his three children destitute. Mrs. Smith found work in a theatre. They wanted a child super in a hurry. Mrs. Smith secured the job for little

Gladys. Her golden hair, her soft blue eyes, her intelligence, and her amiability endeared her alike to audience and company. Within the year, all three Smith children were "trouping." "Smith" would not do for programmes and posters. So they borrowed a family name of an Irish ancestress and became Mary, Lottie, and Jack Pickford.

There followed years of cheap theatrical boarding houses, of lessons learned and recited on trains, of crises in towns which enforced the labour laws against child actors, of ups and downs, until the accidents of the road led Mrs. Smith and her brood to the great theatrical mart in New York. There, by the bold device of invading the stage during a rehearsal, Mary got a child part in Belasco's production, *The Warrens of Virginia*, and scored a modest hit. But child parts are scarce, and Mary had become chief breadwinner of the family. An experienced actress who had appeared under the great Belasco on Broadway would never have tainted her professional reputation with the moving pictures. But Mary was young, inexperienced. When the bank account began to shrink, she applied to Griffith for work. He gave her a "try out"; showed the developed film to his directors. They objected that her head was too large. "A good fault; that's the organ we ought to do things with in this business," Griffith replied. He cast her at once and realized within the first week that he had a prize—temperament, expression, intelligence, beauty, and, above all, a sweet worker.

When Griffith went to Biograph as a director the company was running at a slight deficit. Within two years it paid 1100 per cent. on the investment. It was not alone in its prosperity. All the other Trust companies began to flourish, to boom. And there—progress stopped. The newspapers were talking of the "movie craze," stating in that one contemptuous phrase their skepticism. The cool directing heads of the Trust could not believe that the bonanza was really going to last, nor imagine that beyond their rich island lay a continent of incredible richness—a major American industry. Better let well enough alone! All the directors, and especially Griffith, were yelling for more length. One reel—fourteen or fifteen minutes—was not long enough to tell a good story. The management stood firm.

Taking things into his own hands, Griffith produced a two-reeler entitled *His Trust*. When he showed it at the studio, the chiefs of his company refused flatly to put it out. "Then I quit!" roared Griffith.

Peace makers intervened, and effected a compromise. Biograph sent forth the picture, but as two separate weekly releases—the first entitled *His Trust*, the second *His Trust Fulfilled*. As time went on, these brief serials—one reel to the instalment—became more and more common. Then exhibitors here and there began combining two instalments of the serial into one performance. This opened the way to the two-reeler. But there the Trust dug in and held fast. This tendency of directors to string out their stories was getting dangerous!

As the struggle between artists and management went on someone invented a convincing psychological argument for keeping down footage. The human mind and the human eye, he said, were so constituted that audiences could not keep their attention fixed on a screen narrative for more than twenty minutes. Beyond that, they would lose interest.

Also, the Trust closed its eyes to one primary rule in showmanship. Generally, it refused to advertise its actors, even to let their names appear on the screen or the posters. The product went forth as a Biograph picture, a Vitagraph picture, an Edison picture. Theatrical managers had learned better three hundred years before. We know much about Burbage, the histrionic genius of the Globe Theatre, London, because his auditors were interested in him and recorded his doings. We know much less about Shakespeare, its writing genius, because most of his contemporaries had only a mild interest in the author of the play. Still less were they interested in who owned or managed the theatre.

The main staple which the manager or producer sells

to an ordinary audience is a personality. The inventions of playwrights, the devices of stage managers merely serve to throw this personality into interesting situations. And the cheaper and less sophisticated the audience, the truer the rule. Highbrows and scholars may go to see Shaw or Ibsen; the populace goes to see John Barrymore or Ed Wynn. But the magnates of the moving-picture Trust never admitted this. Also, they feared the effect of publicity on their actors. Advertise them, get them swell-headed and up-stage, and they would demand more salary—perhaps even the undreamed-of salaries paid on the "legitimate" stage, where stars sometimes cost a thousand dollars a week. Mary Pickford did some of her most effective work for Biograph at a salary of fifty dollars; and to the end of her service there, the public knew her only as "The Biograph Girl," or "Little Mary, the Movie Girl with the Curls."

It is easy, in view of what happened afterward, to laugh at their shortness of vision. But they were pioneers, and those who break ground can seldom imagine the harvest. And their eventual rivals, the theatrical managers, were worse than short-sighted: they were blind. Any experienced Broadway showman, it seems now, might have taken hold on the "picture" business and, by applying the basic principles of his own craft, transformed it. But Broadway ignored its existence, even when, in the space of two years, the moving-picture houses of the United States rose in numbers from 300 to 3,000, and road companies of the spoken drama began to fade out.

Even before Griffith and Mary Pickford arrived, the Biograph had established itself in a revamped old mansion at 11 East Fourteenth Street, a stone's throw from the Comedy Theatre. The grand ballroom served as a studio and the bedrooms for laboratories or projecting rooms. In the basement dining rooms the actors and mechanics used to eat their put-up lunches. Thither Mary Pickford walked every day from her boarding house on East Twenty-first Street; thither, presently, came Dorothy and Lillian Gish, whom Griffith singled out from the extra girls for supporting parts and small bits.

Griffith would throw a one-reel film together in two or three days. Finished, he witnessed a "rough run" in his crude projecting room, gave his assistant notes on the cutting, and passed to the next job. The actor who wanted to see himself on the screen had usually to wait until his picture appeared at the exhibiting houses. Mary Pickford learned one afternoon that her latest film, which she had not seen, was running at the Comedy. It was a rush season; Griffith had ordered a night session. By omitting dinner, Mary Pickford could see it at its "supper turn." She repaired to the Comedy, bought a ticket. Al Kaufmann stopped her at the door.

Mary Pickford in The Poor Little Rich Girl

Daniel Frohman

"How old are you?" he asked suspiciously.

"Fifteen," replied Mary. ("I was only fourteen," she says now, "but I saw what was coming, so I lied just a little.")

"Then I can't let you in," said Al Kaufmann. "Children under sixteen not admitted unless accompanied by parents or guardians."

"But I'm from the Biograph Company. I'm the star in the picture you're showing to-night. Look at it— if you have eyes!" said Mary, her Irish starting up.

Al Kaufmann surveyed her. "Sure you are!" he said, "The Biograph girl with the curls. But just the same, I can't let you in. The police are getting awful strict. Suppose you go home and get your mother?"

"Here I'm missing dinner to see my show," said Mary, "and we're called up again for eight. Do you think I've time to walk up to Twenty-first Street and get my mother and walk 'way back again?"

"Then there's nothing doing!"

"Where's the owner of the theatre?"

"It's no use calling for him. He'd tell you the same. We aren't taking any risks with those reformers."

Now Mary's Irish spilled over.

"I want you to understand one thing," she said over her shoulder, "I'm never coming to this house again. Never, never, never!"

She kept her word. When during her term of service in the Biograph she found time and inclination to see herself on the screen, she patronized the Penny Arcade next door.

So she missed her first opportunity of meeting Adolph Zukor, with whom she was to mount the heights of wealth and renown. During her term of service on East Fourteenth Street she never knew that he existed. Years later, she identified him as a pleasant, unobtrusive man who, when she was "working," used often to stand with the knot of spectators back of the lights and the camera.

Again, Adolph Zukor was learning a trade.

CHAPTER XII

ZUKOR PLOTS HIS FUTURE

WHEN the picture theatres which he owned in partnership with Brady began to return their twenty per cent. dividends, Zukor branched out for himself and opened two or three small houses in the poorer districts of New York. These also prospered. The tide of his affairs was flowing serenely again. He likes to live expansively; at every period of his fluctuating fortunes he had adjusted his outgo to his income. Now, he moved his family to better quarters, employed a maid, put Eugene and Mildred into a private school. He had been an athlete in his youth, and that compact, perfectly controlled little body of his had begun of late to cry out for some exercise more strenuous than walking. On one of his vacations in the Catskills he came for the first time into intimate contact with lawn tennis. The game fascinated him. He joined a club on Long Island; and although he began too late to endanger McLaughlin or Johnston, he worked up a passable game.

Marcus Loew, who went into the business of exhibition at about the same time and through the same curious circumstances, had in the meantime far outrun him; for Loew started without the handicap of the moribund Hale's Tours. Parallel with the picture craze ran the vaudeville craze. Loew was riding both the tides, but at this stage of his career, he rather favoured vaudeville. This, to the mind of the Broadway theatrical manager, removed the curse of the moving picture and gave him some standing in the world of illusions. Presently, his store shows sprinkled the city. Next, he advanced the status of the whole business by acquiring the Cosy Corner Theatre in Brooklyn, and turning it into a vaudeville-and-moving-picture house. The Loew heirs say that this was the first real theatre to pass into the hands of the moving picture. Perhaps this assertion might not bear investigation. But at any rate, it was the first in greater New York, which then even more than now dictated dramatic fashions to all America.

By 1910, Loew and Zukor found that they had certain interests in common. Vaudeville talent, for example, was in demand. Neither of them owned enough houses to keep a "feature" busy the whole year. Cheap but promising talent was forever escaping to the provinces or the larger circuits. Zukor, Loew, and one or two smaller exhibitors could, if combined, run an all-year circuit of their own. So in 1910 was formed the Loew Company, with Marcus Loew president and Adolph Zukor nominal treasurer. Into it Zukor threw all his houses except the three he owned with Brady. It paid from the first, even better than had its units.

Now, Zukor seemed to have reached a safe and pleasant haven. "I could have cashed in for between three hundred and five hundred thousand dollars," he says. Better than that, he sat securely at the centre of an expanding business. At his death in 1927, Marcus Loew left a fortune of about $25,000,000. Some of that came from his later enterprises with moving-picture production; but the pith and fibre of it was the chain of "vaudeville-and-picture theatres" which he stretched in the next fifteen years across the United States. Had Zukor transferred all his eggs to that one basket and kept them there, he would have acquired in the course of years a fortune beyond the dreams of an orphan emigrant from sleepy little Ricse.

So much for the externals. But the factor important to this story is what Adolph Zukor's mind was doing in the period between 1907, when he cleaned up the indebtedness of the Hale's Tours Company, and 1912, when he threw dramatically on the table his hazard of new fortunes.

Having entered the moving-picture business with full belief in its future, he set about to learn it in all its departments. When, timidly and apologetically, he asked Griffith if he might watch his casts and cameramen work, the mechanics and extras about the studio thought that he was merely another fascinated loafer, come to look at the pretty girls. As unobtrusive as a piece of studio machinery, he loitered day after day on the outskirts, noting how actors and directors produced their effects, studying lights and scenery. Now and then, he buttonholed an actor or a mechanic and asked a condensed, pointed question. . . . Of nights, he got out his old favourites of classical literature, like *Pilgrim's Progress* or *The Three Musketeers*, and experimented with turning them into moving-picture scenarios.

Frank Meyer had come on from St. Louis to direct a film agency in Fourteenth Street. The Comedy was one of the best customers. For two years, he thought that Al Kaufmann owned the house. Then one day the little man who really owned it came out of his den, introduced himself, began subtly to cross-examine him.

Still further: Zukor spread his education to include the "legitimate" theatre. His partnership gave him the entrée to the busy Broadway offices of William A. Brady; eventually, he had uptown desk-room there. When Jessie Bonstelle sold her stage version of *Little Women* to Brady, Adolph Zukor bought a moderate partnership in the production.

"I felt that the play would go," he says, "and it did. But I was really investing the money in my education."

He took small shares in one or two other Brady ventures which did not do so well. But he achieved his main object. He was studying the spoken theatre, with its background of three centuries; drawing on the accumulated experience of its managers in pleasing and alluring the public. And he was comparing it with the careless yet ossified methods of the moving-picture producers.

There came a dramatic moment when William A. Brady discovered how much Zukor had learned. Brady says now, "Broadway got me for a while." He had been paying more attention to the stock market than to the business of producing plays. One or two failures—and then came a crisis. Down the Great White Way ran the report that Bill Brady had gone broke. Creditors heard the whisperings and pressed in upon him. Brady, buckling down to his own business at last, struck a hasty balance between assets and liabilities and found himself cornered. There seemed no way out except bankruptcy.

Enter now this unconsidered hanger-on of the Brady offices.

"It looks bad, Billy," said Adolph Zukor.

"It looks rotten," said Brady, "but how do you know?"

"I've got eyes, haven't I?" replied Adolph Zukor. "Well, it isn't so bad as it looks. You've been neglecting this business, and certain people have taken advantage of you."

Half of that night they sat in the office with the books. And as they talked, wonder grew in Brady. This partner in his little Fourteenth Street side-show knew more about the Brady business—all of it—than Brady knew himself. There was, for example, one pressing debt of

$90,000. "I've been watching that fellow," said Zukor. "You owe him about $30,000. The rest—it's just taking unfair advantage."

Before they went to bed, Zukor had offered to go through the books and see exactly what could be done. Working fourteen hours a day, he made a digest of the Brady affairs so acute and yet so simple that Brady asked him once where and when he learned accounting. "Nowhere and never," replied Zukor. This statement showed that if they could adjust certain false and fancy charges, like that item of $90,000, the assets would amount to seven eighths of the liabilities. Zukor volunteered to make the adjustment. He succeeded so well that in a week Brady was going ahead with his plans for autumn productions as though nothing had happened. He had two or three successes that year. They put him onto his feet, and he never lost his balance again.

"You deserve a partnership, Adolph," said Brady one day. "You can have it if you want."

Zukor blushed. That is the one manifestation of his inner sentimentalism which his native reserve has never managed to inhibit. But he answered merely:

"Much obliged, Billy. I have other plans!"

Theatrical management never attracted him. His connection with Brady was only a means to an end. The focus of his activities remained that little, crowded playhouse in Union Square, become for him a kind of experimental laboratory. Still he stood at the entrance when the crowds emerged, picking up conversation with typical auditors, asking what they liked about the show. More and more often it was the film.

There came at last an Imp two-reeler entitled *Under the Sea*, which for story and technical effect he felt excelled anything he had ever shown before. That week, his gossips at the door never so much as mentioned the vaudeville acts. All talked of the film. When a one-reel version of *Camille* appeared in the catalogues, Zukor used it for an experiment. He took a versatile young vaudeville performer, who became afterward famous as Lowell Sherman, stationed him in a box beside the screen, and had him talk off, in four "voices," the appropriate dialogue. As in most early attempts to synchronize voice and vision, the result seemed somehow unnatural; Zukor abandoned that.

Always he had doubted the superstition that an audience could not keep its attention on more than two reels of film. In 1910, he had a chance to prove his skepticism. Europeans, who held no preconceived notions on the practical length of a moving-picture film, had reproduced the Passion Play at Oberammergau in three reels. Zukor ventured to buy it, at exceptional prices, for the New York, Boston, and Newark houses. Soberly and appropriately advertised at the Comedy, it drew full houses for a double run. No need this time to

ask the audience what they thought of the film—a third
of them were crying as they emerged. When he passed
the Passion Play on to his Newark house, Zukor experimented further. He installed an organ and accompanied
the film with a programme of sacred music. So far as he
knows, that was the first appearance of the organ in collaboration with the moving picture. A packed house was
filing through the exits when a priest accosted Zukor.

"This show must stop," he said. "It is irreverent. I
propose to see the city authorities and have your licence
withdrawn." Newark licensed its film houses only from
week to week. The city fathers, who had lived through
bitter experiences with certain improper free-lance
films, would refuse a renewal on complaint of almost
any reputable citizen. This, then, was no empty threat.

"But why?" asked Zukor. "If it does them good?
Look at those people coming out. They're crying!"

"That's perfectly true," replied the priest. "It's a
beautiful picture. But a common moving-picture theatre
is no place for it."

Zukor, finding himself unable to argue the subtleties
of Christian theology and sentiment, looked his man
over. He had a kind Irish face; under that must burn
an Irish heart. Zukor struck at this joint in the armour.

"I'm just a little exhibitor," he said. "And I've paid
more for this film than I've ever paid for any other. I've
tried to do it respectfully. Look at those posters there.
Look at the organ. I hadn't any idea of hurting your

feelings or the feelings of your church. I thought I'd
please you. If you get my licence withdrawn—and you
can do it—I won't say you'll quite ruin me, but you'll
hit me a hard blow."

The priest's face worked for a moment. Publicans
and sinners . . . And the greatest of these is charity. . . .

"All right, my boy," he said at length. "I think I
won't report you!"

Adolph Zukor had proved one point to himself. An
audience would sit fascinated through three reels. "But
this is an exception," said the doubting Thomases.
"Religion and all that . . ." Zukor's common sense
told him better. Religion is not the strongest interest
of the theatre. If that were so, Broadway would be
showing miracle plays and mystery plays instead of
sex and melodrama.

Longer films, as well as better films—this idea grew
in his mind to the point of obsession. All his group in
Fourteenth Street, especially Frank Meyer and Al
Kaufmann, became converts and disciples. Once, en-
thused to the point of action, Meyer and Kaufmann
visited Morris Kohn and invited him to back them in
the production of long films. Kohn liked the idea.
But just then his own affairs were tangled; he could not
raise the ready money for such a venture. Apparently
Zukor did not yet dare entertain the idea of producing
himself. For all his pluck, his valorous attitude toward
life, he has a humble mind. This manifests itself often

in doubt of his own powers. If he began producing longer and better films let it be with some established firm which knew the ropes.

In 1910, the Loew consolidation having rendered his affairs temporarily secure, Zukor took his family for another vacation in Europe. Carl Laemmle abode that summer in Wiesbaden. He, with his "Imp" Company, was one of the leading and progressive independents. For the time had come when these free lances, entrenched behind a barrier of legal points, were rising to order and respectability. Zukor travelled from Paris to Wiesbaden in order to unload his idea. Laemmle listened, and half agreed. But the time, he felt, had not yet come. Before attempting anything so large and expensive, they must establish more firmly their legal position.

Refused by the independents, Zukor tried the Trust. When he returned to New York he managed by persuasion and diplomacy to get an appointment with J. J. Kennedy, its genius and driving spirit. Banker, engineer, and fine old Irish gentleman, Kennedy had found himself in a position where it was necessary to fight. And fight he did, with fists and teeth and toenails, until the independents regarded him as a sinister menace and the regulars as a crowned hero. He bestrode the moving-picture world like a colossus. Zukor, himself only a tiny, insignificant figure in the business, felt properly thrilled and awed. As when he found it necessary to persuade his guardian that he must emigrate, he lay awake of nights and scribbled by day in composing a selling talk. Promptly at ten, the hour of the appointment, he reported in Kennedy's outer office.

For more than two hours, the warder of greatness kept him waiting while the musty petitioners of the moving-picture houses filed in and out of that sanctum. When finally she admitted Zukor, Kennedy was tired; also he had an early luncheon engagement. And this, it seemed, was only another "nut" with some fantastic idea to improve the moving picture. For diplomacy's sake, he must listen to a dozen such every week. While Zukor delivered himself, Kennedy watched the clock. The interview ended in a polite dismissal. Mr. Zukor's idea was interesting, very interesting. Some day, when affairs were running more smoothly, the Trust might take the matter up again, consider it seriously. . . .

Zukor found himself in the outer office, nursing a sense of bafflement.

But it drove him back on himself. It crystallized his amorphic determination to enter production on his own account. Night after night he covered the streets of New York with his quick, neat pace of a frontiersman, thinking it out. And by the end of the year 1911, he had a plan and a programme from which, when the moment of action came, he never much deviated.

His producing company would make "full-length" films—a whole evening's entertainment. That was the governing principle. And, having made such films, it would exhibit them so far as possible in first-class theatres on a parity with the legitimate stage. To succeed on this scale, they must excel not only in length but in quality anything that Trust or independents had ever done before. But American films were improving; Zukor could feel a rising tide which must somehow, somewhere break the barriers. Already the business had developed much talent which might go far if given its head. Such directors as Porter, Griffith, and Dawley were chafing at the limitations imposed upon them by men who would never understand—praying for a chance. Actors, real actors who understood the technique of the screen, had begun to emerge from the ruck; not only Mary Pickford but Costello, the Gish sisters, and "Bronco Billy." They, too, quarrelled with the trivial scraps of story which they were given to interpret, and above all with their forced anonymity.

As for the vital basis of this trade—the story—producers had been working with thirty-dollar scenarios. And there were the wonder-stories of twenty centuries and twenty races awaiting interpretation by this new medium. To Zukor, as I have said before, the mode of telling a story, whether by prose, poetry, drama, or pantomime, is immaterial. His mind darts to the essential, even when he considers art. Only, to translate and adapt great stories from one medium to the other would take brains. Well-skilled dramatists, expert story-tellers crowded Broadway. Some of them, if you made the rewards attractive enough, would learn the trick.

This was his working theory; the basis of his plan. It looks obvious now. So, to the mediæval Spanish peasant or the ancient Irish kern, gazing at the Atlantic, it should have seemed obvious that these waters had a Western shore. . . .

But first, you must give this business some dignity; wipe away that contempt in which the American public held the "movie"; kill the slum tradition. In the very institution which had been the vessel of scorn he saw the instrument of rehabilitation—the legitimate stage. If the stage relented, the public would follow. Present some recently successful Broadway drama in film with the original actors, and the prejudice would begin to falter; present a succession of them, and it would die. Stars and dramatists had probably no aversions to the film which money would not overcome. And one night, meditating in his office before a scratch-pad, he put down the motto which his banners bore in so many subsequent years of battle—"Famous Players in Famous Plays."

This, however, was to be not a means but an end. He appreciated the subtle difference between stage acting and screen acting. The talent which would make the business great must come eventually not from Broadway but from Fourteenth Street. "Famous Players in Famous Plays" would be merely a bridge between two eras. After the sensational rise of the film-trained Mary Pickford, after Zukor entered this third and last stage of his programme, critics said that it all came about accidentally; that Zukor, working the thin placer streak of the legitimate stage, stumbled upon the mother-lode. From his old confidants of this brain-ridden period, I know better. He planned it from the first.

It would take money, more money than any producer had ever dreamed of spending on the films. To get Broadway stars he must pay better than Broadway prices. He intended, of course, to kill the old anonymity of screen actors, to advertise and exploit them after the fashion of Broadway managers. That would involve big overhead charges. Night after night he covered his scratch-pad with figures. He must throw in everything he had—and more. He planned to form at least a temporary partnership with some Broadway manager whose prestige would draw the star actors and give the stamp of respectability. He could hardly expect this partner, taking chances with his reputation, to add to the obligation by investing money. There remained only the banks.

Ever since he entered the amusement business, he had deposited with the Irving National Bank; Vice-President Lee, who attended to loans, had become in the course of years his esteemed personal friend. This credit expert, skilled in weighing the honesty and ability of men, had, it seemed, perceived the genius for affairs in this small Fourteenth Street exhibitor. Zukor unloaded his idea in full—laid all his cards on the table. Laughed out of court by his own trade, he found a hospitable mind in the outsider. Lee came to believe in the plan, as he believed already in its author. He promised reasonable credits.

Zukor was drawing a full breath to take the leap, when luck hurled him—somewhat prematurely—over the verge.

CHAPTER XIII

ENTER SARAH BERNHARDT

ℰDWIN S. PORTER, he who produced *The Great Train Robbery*, was working in 1912 as director of the Rex Company, leading independents. With Griffith and Dawley, he stood perhaps at the head of his profession. Though business policy held him down to one- and two-reelers, he enjoyed such merited reputation that Rex, alone of all the independents, had been invited to accept licence from the Trust—and had declined with sarcastic thanks. Zukor, in process of getting his education with the motion picture, visited the Rex studios; on the strength of his burning admiration for *The Great Train Robbery* he struck up an acquaintance with its director. When the idea of longer and better films began to mount to an obsession, he talked it all over with Porter. The director proved more than sympathetic. He was himself railing at the limitations of the one-reeler.

Europe, as I have said before, had no superstitions about the practical length of moving-picture films. Nor did the legitimate stage, over there, regard it with scorn. At this very moment, the Italians were preparing to produce in five or six reels *Cabiria*, a tale of ancient Rome

154

whose sheer beauty no subsequent film has much excelled. In France, the aged Sarah Bernhardt had turned
on this new medium of expression her flame-like intelligence. It exorcised, she told the Parisian reporters, that
old curse on the actor's art—its impermanence. When
the cameramen persuaded her to stand model for two
or three short films, she said: "This is my one chance for
immortality." *Queen Elizabeth*, a drama described by its
title, was her last full-length play. Old, so lame that she
must needs invent new stage business to conceal her
painful limp, she played it nevertheless with all her accustomed fire. As this play began to run down, Louis
Mercanton, a Parisian producer, filmed it in four reels.
He brought to bear the best photography and lighting
that France knew; Bernhardt, an artist in every fibre,
planned its adaptation to the film. Technically, it excelled any previous effort. And Bernhardt, with her definite features, her wealth of expression, and her mastery
of gesture, screened well.

Already there was considerable traffic in films back
and forth across the Atlantic. While the little houses of
France, Belgium, and Italy dressed up their programmes
with "Westerns," the Europeans long held the favourable balance of trade. For one thing, they were making
better films. Then, too, the Trust, having few European
patents, granted licence on request to European films.
Free-lance exhibitors and agents were already taking
advantage of this loophole. Frank Brockliss, an Ameri-

can engaged in the primitive business of distributing moving pictures abroad, saw the show in London. The American rights were going begging. He wrote all this to Joseph Engel of the Rex Company. Engel told Porter, who saw that it fitted exactly into Zukor's programme. Porter passed the word along. Before it reached Zukor, Engel had bought an option on the American rights. Zukor called him up on the telephone.

"It's the greatest feature ever presented in America," said Engel.

"They always are," replied Zukor. "How much do you want?"

"Thirty-five thousand dollars," said Engel; "half down, the balance when the returns come in."

Zukor's next words almost caused Engel to drop the telephone receiver. He had quoted a top price, expecting to haggle. And this small exhibitor had answered:

"All right, I'll take it."

For Zukor, on his part, was actually afraid that *Queen Elizabeth* would slip out of his hands. From the moment when Porter's message reached him, he perceived that this was a Heaven-sent opportunity. He wanted to establish the habit of long films. This ran the unprecedented length of four reels. He wanted to give the motion picture respectability by dragging into its scope the big figures of the stage. And here came Bernhardt.

Perhaps a historian of those times must inform the

young reader that Bernhardt occupied in the international theatre a position such as no actor has ever held before or since. She was more than queen of the stage; she was its empress, almost its goddess. France had loaded on her all the honours of the Republic. When she made her farewell tour of America, the Players, oldest and most traditional of actors' clubs, broke its rule against admitting women except on Ladies' Day, and gave her a reception. Bernhardt was above all rules. Now let the minor luminaries scorn the motion picture!

Before two days, the news had saturated the motion-picture business; by the week-end it had reached the provincial, nervous, gossiping circle of Broadway. Zukor, said Fourteenth Street, had bought that high-brow Bernhardt film for thirty-five thousand dollars— which rumour presently exaggerated to fifty thousand. He'd been talking a little crazily of late. He must have gone clean over the line! Broadway joined in the laugh. It was the first time that most of the gossips, passing the joke through the theatrical clubs and the white-light bars, had ever heard the name of Adolph Zukor.

Busy days now; too busy to dwell on the desperate chances he was taking! For Adolph Zukor was not putting forth *Queen Elizabeth* as a mere experiment. He had passed that stage. When years later someone asked him the old, bromidic question, "To what do you attribute your success?" he answered: "I merely rode a tide." The motion picture was ready to break through artificial barriers. As soon as *Queen Elizabeth* proved to the motion-picture world that an audience could keep its attention on a long film and to the theatrical world that the camera did not taint the reputation of a star, a dozen others, with financial resources such as he could never command, might start from the mark.

While he waited for the little tin cylinders to arrive by mail steamer, he took a modest office in the Times Building which towered symbolically over the theatrical district, and incorporated the Famous Players Company. In the past two years he had thought everything out, even to the details of his personal life. To be prosperous on Broadway you must look prosperous. He bought at once his first motor car, and moved from his modest flat to an apartment in West Eighty-eighth Street where there was room and equipment for entertaining. Then he began search for a partner and chaperon—some established theatrical manager.

Old friendship as well as his judgment of men led him first to the popular, expansive, and venturesome William A. Brady. He got a hearing, of course; the rescue of the business was still gratefully fresh in Brady's memory. Zukor, in the days when he talked "longer and better films" to any listener, had unloaded his ideas on his partner. He needed only to add that the *Queen Elizabeth* film gave him an exceptional, a providential opening.

But Brady shook his head. "Adolph, I'm just on my

feet again, thanks to you," he said. "Besides," he added, "when I married Grace George, I promised I'd stop promoting prize fights."

Zukor took this last for the joke that it was. But he answered: "You won't feel that way about it in two years, Billy."

"Perhaps not," said Brady. Then he grew serious. "I want to stand on what I said, nevertheless. There's a time to take chances and a time to pull in and go slow. Of course, you've done more for me than any other man alive. . . ." ("And when I said this," remarked Brady fifteen years later, "he looked as shy as a girl getting her first proposal.") "I'll tell you what I'll do though; if you can't get anyone else, I'll stand by you—of course."

"Much obliged," said Zukor, "but I am thinking of trying Dan Frohman."

"Dan Frohman!" exclaimed Brady, and gave an incredulous whistle.

It did look a little preposterous. At that moment, the Frohman brothers, Charles and Daniel, stood with Belasco as chief pillars of the artistic theatre. They, if anyone, had a right to look down from the pinnacles of Broadway on the fens and dumps of Fourteenth Street. But Zukor had a fortunate opening to their attention. When the small exhibitors formed the Loew Company, Elek J. Ludvigh became its attorney. He also represents that Hungarian strain so powerful in the modern motion-picture business. He was born in New York a year after his parents emigrated from Hungary. By one of those matrimonial alliances which clutter this story, he had become cousin-in-law to the Frohmans. At Zukor's request, he had seen Dan Frohman and planted the seed. William Morris, the vaudeville manager, added his good offices.

Zukor picked Dan Frohman rather than Charles for sound but various reasons. The Frohman brothers were not a partnership; they had kept their separate identities. At the moment Charles, what with the success of Barrie and Maud Adams, soared high; while Daniel, to express the situation in the dialect of Broadway, had "pulled off a string of flops." He was at the nadir of his career; in the mood for a hazard of new fortunes. Also, Daniel Frohman has the golden gift of friendship. Men and women both like him on sight for his easy geniality, his wit, and his heart. His romantic quarters above the Lyceum Theatre are plastered with the photographs of stage people from Bernhardt and Irving down to humble understudies; and their autographed dedications seem to ring with affectionate appreciation. The circle of his friendships extended beyond his own profession to the other arts. Most usefully, he was on house-guest terms with some of the most popular authors of the period.

Though Daniel Frohman, with his capacity for absorbing gossip, had heard of Zukor, it was their first meeting. After some shy preliminaries, Zukor opened

Sarah Bernhardt in Queen Elizabeth, *the first poster ever made for the Famous Players Film Company*

The old Twenty-sixth Street studio rebuilt. This photograph was taken after the top of the building containing the studio had been rebuilt, following the fire

br/>

up his mind and talked as he can when he comes to
the crux of a situation—clearly, logically, all data di-
gested, all contingencies foreseen. Frohman began to
like him, and gave hospitable attention. Zukor had
guessed shrewdly on the state of his worldly affairs.
"I'm in a venturesome mood," said Frohman. "Probably I'm going to take you up. But I can't put in any
money."

That was a minor disappointment; Zukor had hoped
for a little accession to his slender capital. But the
Frohman name and influence were the main thing, after
all. In that one session, they struck a bargain. Frohman,
for his services and his name, was to receive a block of
stock in the company. "Gambling my fair reputation
against a fortune," he said.

That night he broke the news to his brother. Charles
had a crusty side. "He couldn't have been more dis-
gusted," writes Terry Ramsaye, "if his brother had
opened a hot-dog stand at Coney Island."

Daniel Frohman established a desk in the little office
of the Times Building and began to circulate through his
world. Zukor, by way of raising capital, sold most of his
outside enterprises except his share in the Loew Company. Then he set himself to gathering a working staff.
Al Kaufmann, who had risen with him and shared his
enthusiasm, was to be production manager—his re-
ward the same salary which he got as manager of the
Comedy, plus a share in the business. On like terms,

Frank Meyer, who had a bent for applied science, took service as mechanical superintendent. Zukor intended to exploit his stars on theatrical terms; he needed a good press agent. Ben Schulberg, then advertising agent for the independent Rex Company, had come favourably to his attention as a young man of force and energy. Ever since the films began modestly to exploit themselves, Schulberg had starred in moving-picture journalism—always on the independent side. He was receiving fifty dollars a week, and troubling the management weekly with appeals for a raise. Porter sent him to Zukor; and in the little office of the Times Building he faced for the first time that spruce figure, those kindly but inscrutable hazel eyes.

"I want to offer you a job," said Zukor. "Porter, I believe, has told you the details. What are you drawing down from Rex?"

"Fifty dollars a week," replied Schulberg. "But I've good prospects there, and besides it's an established firm. Your scheme is a long chance. I'd expect to be paid for giving up a sure thing."

"How much?"

"Two hundred dollars a week," said Schulberg, inhibiting an impulse to gulp.

"Are you a gambler?" asked Zukor.

"What do you mean—gambler?"

"I mean I'm not going to offer you any better salary than you're getting. But I'm going to ask you to gamble with me—and I'll pay for the chips. I'll give you fifty dollars a week and two hundred shares of stock in Famous Players. You know how big this thing is going to be if it succeeds. If it fails, it will fail just as big. Meantime—you'll be making as good a salary as you get from Rex."

"Which will go up if the company gets prosperous?" enquired Schulberg.

"Oh, certainly!"

All his life, Schulberg had longed for a little capital. Two hundred shares in anything seemed a glittering prospect. He accepted, and left the office wondering if he was really a good gambler or only a bedazzled fool.

A stroke of luck with human material completed the office force. All this time, Zukor and his associates were distributing *Queen Elizabeth*. For this purpose he had formed the temporary Enghandine Company; to describe the complexities of this business would only clog my narrative. They needed a good "road" salesman to deal with the interior cities; and none good enough seemed momentarily available in the business itself. By now, Schulberg had begun by diplomacy and device to sprinkle trade journals and general newspapers with news of "Famous Players in Famous Plays."

Back from the road came Alexander Lichtmann. He, like all others who created the new era of the film, reached the business from much coming and going on the earth. He had been a barnstorming actor, a private in the United States Army, and finally had stumbled into film salesmanship. Underneath the fulsome notices of the Famous Players he sensed a desperate gamble. He liked that. He called on Zukor, "sold himself." The preliminary orders for *Queen Elizabeth* had gone so badly as to cause Zukor considerable worry. Al Lichtmann infused the project with new life. To finish with this part of the business: the enterprise paid in dollars and cents, adding something to Zukor's carefully guarded capital. Also, it fulfilled its primary purpose. The states' rights buyers, coached and persuaded by the resourceful, energetic Lichtmann, adopted the policy of reselling for exhibition in regular theatres at theatrical prices. In one stroke, it opened for the motion picture a channel from the slums to the heart of cities.

Meantime, on July 12, 1912, Zukor and Frohman exhibited *Queen Elizabeth* in New York. Frohman had persuaded his brother, now melting a little toward this daring new departure, to grant the use of the sacrosanct Lyceum Theatre for a special invitation matinee performance. This setting alone gave it the seal of dramatic respectability. In July, almost all Who's Who in New York have fled to the seashore or to Europe. Nevertheless, dozens of literary, artistic, and dramatic figures came back for the day to the hot city "just to help Dan out"; the list of names made a brave showing in next day's notices. There came also the lords of the motion picture. A minority, arguing out the matter in the lobbies, called it a historic occasion. An audience had sat entranced through four reels; had at the end applauded as though Bernhardt were present in the flesh. The longer and more expensive film—already denominated the "feature"—was on the way. But the majority, including officials of the Trust, said that Bernhardt was Bernhardt; when this fellow Zukor tried it with ordinary actors of ordinary reputation, they saw his finish.

Already Famous Players was producing for itself. Al Kaufmann had selected for studios the two top floors of an old armoury in West Twenty-sixth Street; Frank Meyer had rushed the instalment of working equipment. Shrewdly and generously, Zukor had formed his important artistic staff. Edwin S. Porter, always more interested in the job than in its financial rewards, needed little urging; stock in the company, a modest salary, and a chance at "big" pictures brought him in. J. Searle Dawley, too, jumped at the chance. Zukor wanted Griffith; but Biograph, knowing well what an asset he was, had tied down the pioneer of Fourteenth Street with a contract.

All this time, Frohman was employing his energy, personality, and resourcefulness in rounding up actors and productions. The first to listen to reason was James O'Neill. This age celebrates him as father of our most honoured American playwright. In his own time, all the provinces knew him for his thirty-year run of *The Count of Monte Cristo*, which he had played in glittering opera houses, intimate small-town theatres, circus tents, barns, even the open air. This piece would make a splendid bridge between the famous European players and the famous American players whom the company intended to exploit. James O'Neill seldom played in New York and so he had escaped the Broadway prejudices. The slack summer season was coming on. This offered a chance to make some extra money. He needed little persuading.

Then James K. Hackett listened. He had been in his youth the matinée idol of Broadway. As his hair began to thin and his features to sharpen, he took up Shakespeare and romantic "costume" drama. *The Prisoner of Zenda*, his latest offering, had just finished a long run. Hackett had in him a streak of independence; he rather liked to quarrel with the majority. Also, it was a lark. He and most of his company signed for an immediate production.

The studio forces in West Twenty-sixth Street burst now into activity. In less than two weeks from the first "shot" to the last cutting, Porter filmed a four-reel version of *Monte Cristo*. Then he rushed ahead on *Zenda*. The action involved swimming a moat. This called for a tank. The floor of the old armoury was frail. Frank Meyer found by measure and calculation that it would stand only a foot and a half of water. Even then, he trembled whenever a visitor entered the studio, lest it be a building inspector. When Hackett swam the moat, he crawled on the zinc bottom, giving an imitation of an overhand stroke. The production cost seven thousand dollars—an unprecedented sum.

Frohman was arranging for a "promotional" showing of *Monte Cristo* on Broadway when the opposition hit the new company a sinister jab. Experience had long ago taught the motion-picture business that you cannot keep a studio secret. Too many people of too many sorts are involved in a production—mechanics, cameramen, actors, directors, extras, even the distributing forces, which must know in advance the company's plans. O'Neill had scarcely signed his contract when the gossipy breezes of Broadway carried the news to the governing powers of the motion picture. A Trust firm in Chicago started from the mark with a three-reel version of *Monte Cristo*. Zukor and his associates had adapted the play, which stood protected by copyright. But Dumas's novel, being a classic, was immune from such protection. These rivals made their scenario from the novel direct, and stood scatheless before the law. Just when *Monte Cristo* was titled and ready for transformation into positive prints, the news reached Zukor and Frohman. In both minds it created the same reaction. They could not now put forth *Monte Cristo* as their first American feature. They must begin with a splash, a bang—with the unprecedented feature. This

Chicago version, inferior though it probably was, would take the edge off their production. In one hasty conference they decided to send it to the storehouse for later release, and to substitute *Zenda*.

The initial, promotional showing of *Zenda* came off in the autumn, after Who's Who in New York returned to town. Deliberately Frohman made this an invitation affair and set his showing in the afternoon, when the people of the theatre might attend. He and Hackett drew in all their acquaintances of the artistic clubs and of the stage. Ben Schulberg, publicity agent, had done his job so well that the political and financial celebrities who received invitations deemed this new thing worthy of their attention. Never before had the rays of the motion-picture projector crowned so brilliant an audience. Seldom, indeed, had the spoken stage seen the like. And the picture made an unprecedented hit. Rightly so; spite of the divine Sarah, it came nearer to telling a story, conveying emotion to an audience, even than *Queen Elizabeth*. We should call it archaic and inexpressive nowadays.

Just as the orchestra finished the overture and while the audience was waiting for the curtain, Dan Frohman stepped to the footlights for a little speech.

"Ladies and gentlemen," he said, "I have the honour to announce that the General Film Company has licensed this production. Mr. Zukor has just received the news by telephone."

Leading actors, popular authors, and prominent bankers sat puzzled at the prolonged applause which broke out from spots in the orchestra and balcony. It came from the independent film producers, who alone understood what this announcement signified. Zukor and Frohman had been walking on the edge of disaster; and disaster was now averted, at least temporarily.

CHAPTER XIV

EDISON WRITES A LETTER

WHEN he planned his revolution in the business of making motion pictures, Zukor had faced and acknowledged one cardinal trick. The Trust stood in his way, as in that of every independent with a new idea. "If you can't bust a trust, join it; if you can't join it, bust it," said business men in those days. Zukor cherished no moral abhorrence to trusts. Indeed he preferred that the lords of industry should take him into their circle of nine or ten approved companies. Otherwise, he might expect both a nasty fight involving heavy legal expenses and an artificially restricted market among distributors and exhibitors. To insure himself against this contingency, he had engaged as attorney for his new company the shrewd and theatre-wise Elek J. Ludvigh.

However, he faced the battle with considerable hope. The Trust had of late appealed more and more to public opinion. "We present the best films, and clean films," said its publicity agents. He proposed to offer more ambitious films than the Trust dreamed of. If it refused them licence, it put itself in an illogical position. The enemy might command the heavier battalions, but he had most of the ammunition. Working sixteen hours a day at his complex task of organization, Zukor stored this worry in the cellar of his mind. He would cross the bridge when he came to it.

As he prepared to exploit and exhibit *Zenda*, the bridge began to look more and more like a barrier. Following its precedent, the Trust had licenced *Queen Elizabeth* as a foreign film. *Zenda*, made by an upstart company on American soil, stood in a different category. Ludvigh and Frohman put out feelers, and got no satisfaction either of approval or disapproval. But that incident of a rival *Monte Cristo* gave a sinister indication. The day of *Zenda's* promotional showing arrived; and still the Trust had not spoken. The personnel of the Famous Players entered the Lyceum Theatre that afternoon in a state of tense anxiety. Zukor, looking over the assembling audience, imagined that every male spectator was a process server waiting to tag him with an injunction.

However, the Trust was not holding its peace merely by way of dangling Famous Players on the string. There were divided counsels in its directorate. One minority faction believed with Zukor that refusal of a licence would alienate public opinion. Another had itself been urging longer and better films; it saw in *Zenda*, as in *Queen Elizabeth*, a stimulus from the outside. The Trust, with the inertia of a business grown soggy through prosperity, characteristically delayed

action until the last moment. As the doorkeepers unlocked the Lyceum Theatre for that vital matinee performance, its directors were considering the problem at
luncheon. And the two minorities, acting together, won
the day. They resolved to licence *Zenda*, with the
canny reservation that this action must not be considered a precedent.

One of the directors, appreciating the anxiety
at the Lyceum Theatre, had promised to telephone
news of the final decision. At half-past two the audience
was assembled, but the telephone rang not. At a
quarter of three the house began to grow impatient.

"What shall we do?" whispered Frohman.

"Run it, licence or no licence," responded Zukor.

Then, just as the operator lit up his booth, came the
good news.

So far, so good. But the Famous Players, which intended to produce films continuously, could not go on
through the fogs of such uncertainty. Ludvigh, Frohman, and Zukor began pressure for a continuous licenc-
ing arrangement. The Trust refused to commit itself.
Then Frohman thought of Thomas A. Edison. He it was
who, taking many ideas from many sources and adding
a few of his own, harmonized them to make the practical
moving-picture camera. The American public, indeed,
credited him with the entire invention. So far as he
was still involved in the motion picture, his interests
lay with the Trust. I need not dwell on his personal

prestige. A word from him might melt all opposition. If that failed, and they had to draw the public into the game, his support would be the ace of trumps.

Frohman went over to the laboratory at East Orange, and gained an audience with the Wizard. Into Edison's best ear he poured the story of an enterprise which was going to lift the moving picture to new heights of art, usefulness, and profit. All they needed was a licence. And Edison's influence could accomplish it.

"Well what, speaking specifically, can I do for you?" asked Edison.

"Give me a letter to the Motion-Picture Patents Company, asking them to licence our product," replied Frohman.

Edison pulled up a laboratory scratch-pad, wrote a brief note, handed it to Frohman. As he took it Frohman had to control the trembling of his fingers; and a minute later he was controlling the muscles of his face. It was a coldly formal letter of the kind which a man of affairs writes when he cannot refuse a request and yet does not want to commit himself. As a weapon against the Trust, it was worse than useless. Thinking quickly, Frohman determined to get Edison into a more genial mood before telling him all this. And his mind flew to the past.

"I was Horace Greeley's office boy on the old New York *Tribune*," he began. "And I used to see you when you were a newspaper telegrapher."

Edison started from the mark, recalling old anecdotes of Greeley, Bennett, of dead-and-gone mutual acquaintances, and humorous incidents remembered from his days at the key. Warming up, he passed on to his beginnings as an inventor. Presently he was telling, with some lingering resentment, how a company which controlled an inferior product had killed one of his early inventions. Here was an opening. Frohman wriggled through it for a touchdown.

"Don't you see, Mr. Edison," he interrupted, "that we're exactly in the same fix to-day as you were then?"

"Well, I've written you a letter, haven't I?" inquired Edison. "What more can I do?"

"Make it strong," said Frohman. "Look at it! That won't get us anything."

Edison reread his note and smiled. But he hesitated.

"Exactly the same fix you were in!" repeated Frohman.

"I guess you're right," replied Edison suddenly. "Here goes again."

In the second letter he committed himself definitely to the cause of the Famous Players; asked and advised his associates to grant it every possible favour. Using Edison as a lever, Frohman and Zukor pried from the Trust a permanent licence at the standard fee—half a cent a foot.

So, in a manner of speaking, Zukor entered the Trust. Also—though this was not his intention—he

broke the Trust. Having admitted this exponent of more
ambitious films, it could not in reason refuse licences to
other newcomers with a superior product. From that
time forth, it cut less and less figure in the world of
shadows. The tide of progress had overrun all the
artificial barriers. By 1913 the distinction between
"regulars" and "independents" had grown hazy. By
1915, when the courts finally dissolved the combination, the line had disappeared. Generally, those who
were lords of the motion picture before 1912 retired to
live happily ever after on comfortable fortunes. Leadership of the newer and greater era passed to those who
had been least of their vassals—the little five-cent,
store-show exhibitors and agents of the back streets.
Here the Trust virtually disappears from this story.

The names of Bernhardt and Hackett had made
magic, as expected. The spoken theatre was nodding to
its hoyden cousin. Dan Frohman worked day and night
to shove the movement along. Every fine afternoon he
brought parties of dramatic, social, and literary celebrities to the cluttered studio in West Twenty-sixth
Street and displayed to them the novel spectacle of
films in the making. Some daring débutante asked for
a chance with the extra girls, which Frohman graciously
granted. It became fashionable; certain mobs of the old
Famous Players productions look like a garden party
at Tuxedo. More practically, Frohman was making

headway in securing famous plays and players. Minnie Maddern Fiske does her own thinking. After she saw the studio at work and heard the plan, she agreed to be filmed in *Tess of the D'Urbervilles*, probably her greatest popular success. At that period in his career, John Barrymore regarded the drama lightly; he was always on the point of packing up his costumes and taking to cartooning. A liberal offer brought him in. Lillie Langtry, being British, had no preconceived prejudices; she signed a contract.

Also, Zukor himself had secured Mary Pickford; and fortune so managed the affair that she, above all other actors, bridged for him the gulf between the "movies" and the "legit." When her engagement as Betty in *The Warrens of Virginia* drew to its close, Belasco told her that, while child actresses were but little in demand, she should have the next chance with him. Thereupon, as related, she became the "Girl with the Curls," and "Little Mary" for Biograph. In 1911, Belasco, preparing *The Good Little Devil*, wanted an emotional ingénue for the leading part of the blind girl. He had been watching Mary Pickford's success in the films, noting how she had developed. He engaged her, and *The Good Little Devil* was a major hit of the season. The piece had closed now; and Mary Pickford was in process of deciding between the screen and the footlights when Zukor sent for her. She reports that as she entered the office she saw Al Kaufmann sitting in the corner.

"Oh," she said resentfully, "you're the man who threw me out of your theatre because I was too young to see myself on the film!"

But she listened to Zukor. He intended to buy the screen rights of *The Good Little Devil*, and wanted Mary Pickford as star. "And I mean star," he said. "You'll have your own name on the titles and the paper."

Mary Pickford, who is herself a shrewd bargainer, felt an impulse to close with him at once. However, she choked it back and argued the question. She had made the jump to the legitimate stage, she said; Belasco promised her a great future. She didn't know. . . .

"Would twenty thousand dollars a year salary tempt you?" asked Zukor. "Of course, I don't intend to stop with *The Good Little Devil*. I want you as a steady feature."

Now in all these hard years on the road Mary Pickford had held before the eyes of her imagination one goal. It was to earn twenty thousand dollars a year before she was twenty years old. "I made a little song of it," she says. "'Twenty thousand before I am twenty —twenty thousand before I am twenty!'" That would keep everyone in comfort. Time and again she had rehearsed the items to herself. And here she was, only nineteen!

"It would," she said suddenly. Before she left the office she had signed an agreement.

When they approached Belasco for the rights to

The Good Little Devil he glowed to the proposal. While motion-picture production did not allure him, he had never cherished the conventional prejudice against the film, else he would not have reëngaged Mary Pickford after her long career with the Biograph. Zukor had a daring idea—begin *The Good Little Devil* with Belasco in his study, reading the manuscript of the play while the wraiths of the characters floated past him. With all his own dramatic graciousness, Belasco accepted. And at the moment, he stood to America as the leading exponent of the artistic theatre.

Finally, and somewhat later in the game, Daniel Frohman, strolling one day into his brother's office, stumbled against a financial conference.

"Raise me some ready money at once," Charles was saying to his treasurer. "I've been expanding too fast this season."

Daniel tiptoed out. Returning, he laid a check for $25,000 on his brother's desk.

"What's that for?" enquired Charles.

"An option on the picture rights to all your Barrie productions," said Daniel.

"All right!" replied Charles, without a moment's hesitation. And he dropped the check into a drawer.

The ghost of an old prejudice was forever laid. The footlights at last accepted the screen on terms of social equality. Where the stage led, presumably the public would follow. Zukor had attained his first objective.

CHAPTER XV

THE LOW SPOT

$\mathcal{F}$OR a time, everyone concerned in this new venture was busy and very happy with the glow of initial success. These pioneers remember especially the halcyon nights in Daniel Frohman's suite over the Lyceum Theatre. There, directors, principal actors, and management met to thrash out the work for the next day. That important cog in the moving-picture machine, the "continuity writer," was not yet invented. In collaboration, they hammered theatrical form into motion-picture form—Porter, Dawley, the star of the current feature, Frohman, Zukor, Mrs. Zukor. Usually Mary Pickford came, whether the production was hers or not. Young though she was, she had a sure grasp on the technique of screen acting and screen effects.

Often when the symposium dragged itself out, Frohman sent downstairs for supper and, still absorbed in discussion, they sat until they had to grope their way out of doors through the darkened lobbies; for the performance below had ended hours before. Frohman has in this suite what he calls his "magic box"—a chute which, when the cover is lifted, looks down on the stage of the Lyceum and transmits every accent of the actors.

A group momentarily out of the discussion would sometimes open the magic box and let in distant music of mellow voices speaking Barrie.

Wherever Zukor sits, he becomes eventually head of the table. His, in these discussions, was the final voice. Even the directors admitted that he gave them original suggestions. He arrived tired with an inhuman day's work; but when Mrs. Zukor tried to drag him home, he protested that these symposiums freshened him up. At that period—and even to-day—the actual production of films focussed all his ambitions. His ten hours of managing finances and business details were only preliminary work. When he got Famous Players firmly on its feet, he would proceed to make himself the Belasco of the screen.

Life balked that ambition, continued to balk it. It is his one failure in material achievement. Before Famous Players had been running three months, there came need for genius in financing, direction, and management; and no one else in the combination fulfilled those terms. As in the next few years the screen went on to its unimagined destinies, that need increased. Gradually and reluctantly, Zukor passed from art to finance.

For the tide he was riding had swollen to a point where it threatened to swamp him. That twelvemonth which began in the summer of 1912 had seen the birth of a new screen. Others were following Zukor, even as he anticipated. And the repressed waters had broken through in other places; even the two-reelers began to make history. A young truck horse of the vaudeville stage named Charlie Chaplin accepted with some misgivings a job in motion pictures. Long he produced only one- or two-reelers of the custard-pie-throwing variety, but they excelled all previous film comedy; they are going yet. In that same field of the two-reeler, John Bunny was capitalizing his fat. Bronco Billy had come out of his anonymity under the name of G. M. Anderson, and Maurice Costello, one of the first legitimate actors to enter "pictures," blazed out as a star; in 1912, he headed a Vitagraph company which went round the world, filming as it travelled.

J. Stuart Blackton, perhaps the most able of the old group, had leaped into the long film. As Zukor saw the use of the successful play on the screen, so Blackton perceived the mine of wealth in best-selling novels; at top speed he was transferring Rex Beach and Jack London into five-, six-, and seven-reelers. Griffith, declining another offer from Zukor, was preparing on his own account to produce that epoch-maker, *The Birth of a Nation*, and *Rainey's African Hunt*, in nine reels, had begun to sweep the country.

Others plunged into the long film—firms which produced their one picture and died or firms now solidly encased in the great combinations of Hollywood. The newspapers no longer called the fashion a mere craze: the pioneer film critics made their modest first appearance. "Picture houses" grew in number and pretension. Theatrical managers, routing road shows, more and more commonly found blocks of time in the small-city theatres engaged for this or that feature moving picture.

These are only glimpses of a great, confused revolution; a new, mad industry suddenly upheaving itself from chaos and nothingness. But to Famous Players, coursing breathlessly ahead of the pack which it had started, the situation brought anxiety and perplexity. The film lords of the Trust were right about salaries; as soon as stars saw their names on the programme and the posters they began to demand larger rewards. Even those anonymous indispensables, the cameramen and expert mechanics, were in such demand that a manager must pay high to keep them. Everything was costing more than Zukor expected when he began.

Also, the system of distribution was changing. Later, I will take up that important matter in detail. It is enough to say that a leading firm, to keep in the running, must now produce a continuous supply—even of long films. Eventually, Zukor must furnish, either in combination or alone, two complete films a week for change of programme, or one hundred and four a year. That was unattainable at present; but always circumstances drove him to increase his output. Already it had become impossible to supply the whole demand with pretentious productions like *Zenda* or *The Good Little Devil*.

Zukor prepared to organize his studio forces into

Classes A, B, and C. The A's were the Famous Players in Famous Plays, the B's trained film actors with a reputation, the C's obscure players interpreting hack scenarios. Mary Pickford was long in Class B, though she did not know that until many years later. Eventually, as players like her gained following and reputation, he intended to drop Class A altogether. A few months of actual experience had confirmed his opinion that actors and directors trained in the business itself would eventually hold the heights of Shadowland. The great stars of the "legitimate" were educated and set in another kind of technique. Gesture, posture, and expression which seemed natural behind the footlights appeared strained and forced on the screen. In *The Good Little Devil*, for example, the film version used the exceptionally able company which enacted the spoken original. I saw that old film recently, and Mary Pickford was the only one that I believed. Further, the stage stars generally looked upon the screen only as a rich pot-boiler for slack seasons. They did not put into it their last ounce of energy and interest, as did the regular moving-picture people to whom it was the sole career.

So the scale of his business had increased; but not its resources. Virtually, Zukor had nothing to support this structure except his own little fortune, the profits from those early road shows, *Queen Elizabeth* and *Zenda*, and that abnormal credit of his with the banks. In the modern moving-picture business one must wait long for his money. A firm begins continuous production in January, say; the film can scarcely go forth before June, and it is January again before returns from its sale or distribution reach their peak. Meantime, production, with its heavy expense, is going steadily on. Just before the second January comes the low spot. If you survive until the next June you reach a peak of returns, and all thereafter is well. But that low spot is a slough of despond which has smothered many and many a promising enterprise. Zukor approached it in the summer of 1913. Al Lichtmann, selling states' rights on the road, read a sinister sign in the letters and telegrams from the head office. Early in the week he would flash to New York a low cash offer for a certain piece of territory, and Zukor would spurn it. Thursday or Friday would come a telegram "Accept offer and wire money." This, to Lichtmann's shrewd intelligence, meant only one thing: Zukor was having trouble in meeting his payroll. Once he failed on that—down would come Famous Players like a house of cards.

Other creditors he could put off, was putting off; but his formidable payroll had become a nightmare. Zukor threw everything into the bottomless pit. One week it was the reserve of securities which he was keeping to insure his family against his disposition to gamble with business; already, in the first pinch, he had sold one thousand shares in the Loew Company—these he had been holding against the great multiplication of values which he foresaw. Then he called on Morris Kohn, offering for $25,000 an interest he held in the Penny Arcade business. He had been turning a smiling and inscrutable face to the outer world. Before this relative and old associate, however, he dared let down a little and express his burning anxiety. Kohn, to save time, himself bought the shares for spot cash. Zukor dumped that into the hole.

Then, by that persuasiveness of his, he wheedled the bank into lending him just a little more. But there, Lee informed him, it must stop. While he believed personally in Zukor and his enterprise, he had the directors to reckon with. Probably, from the banking point of view, the time had come to call a halt. In the vaults of two banks lay at that moment more than $200,000 worth of Adolph Zukor's notes, secured by some second-hand machinery and a few films which, if the "craze" collapsed during the next few months, would be only spoiled celluloid. Into the yawning chasm went this last loan. The next week Mrs. Zukor insisted on selling her jewels. That sacrifice of affection, together with some small scrapings from the corners of his empty estate, met the next payroll. Long before, Zukor had considered selling his car and giving up his apartment. But he dismissed that idea. News travels fast on Broadway; and there, of all places, to be prosperous you must look prosperous. If his car disappeared, if he moved to poorer quarters, the pack would be down on him. . . .

Now, he was up against a blank wall. Two weeks ahead lay the turning point; for then payments would begin to roll in. But for all he could see, it might as well lie two centuries ahead. Famous Players was so busy making history that it neglected to record history. Also, fire afterward destroyed what records there were. It is impossible, therefore, to date this crisis exactly. But it came in 1913, and toward the end of the summer.

In the middle of the week Daniel Frohman dropped as usual into the studio. When Zukor said good-morning that pleasant smile of his looked forced. Frohman watched him as he puttered with the papers on his desk. All the lines of his face drooped.

"What's the matter with you, Adolph?" he asked suddenly.

"Nothing," replied Zukor.

"But there is something," persisted Frohman. "Come on, Adolph—tell me!"

Suddenly Zukor's reserve broke down.

"It's the business," he began. And he poured it out in a burst. So much confidence had his associates in Adolph Zukor that even Frohman, the business man, had never thought much about the financial basis of their enterprise. The Chief was taking care of that. After his initial burst of emotion, Zukor sketched the situation coolly and logically. Salvation lay a fortnight ahead; but they must exist meanwhile. He had exhausted every resource, every device. Nothing for it but bankruptcy—his old personal devil—or a receiver. Himself, he would be squeezed out altogether or reduced to a minor position. The control would pass to bankers, who could never understand what Famous Players was trying to accomplish.

"Well, I'll see if I can do anything," said Frohman as he left the office. Adolph Zukor took this sombrely. He was inured to hollow reassurances.

Frohman started to the Lyceum. On the way his intense human sympathies and his ardent belief in the business came together in a benevolent resolution. When he made his first success in theatrical management he had segregated from his earnings enough money to insure him against poverty in his old age; for he knew well the speculative nature of his business. This he invested in first-class bonds, which he tucked away in his safety-deposit box. Through all his vicissitudes he had held this reserve secret and sacred. Suddenly, Frohman changed his course, walked to the bank, to the safety-deposit vaults. . . .

That afternoon, he returned to the studio, and laid on Zukor's desk a check for $50,000.

"It's a loan, not an investment, Adolph," he said. "Pay me when you get out of the woods."

Fourteen years later, Adolph Zukor, dwelling on the virtues of Dan Frohman, came out with this story. He who heard it met Frohman next day and mentioned the incident. Frohman blushed like a girl.

"Did Adolph tell you that?" he faltered. Himself, he had never told.

They passed the "low spot"; although Zukor had to juggle his finances, receipts were now flowing in. Also, Mary Pickford had begun to come into her kingdom. When as a mere child she worked for Biograph, Griffith had usually cast her for parts a little older than her age; at fourteen, she was enacting eighteen. Now, when she had reached twenty and stood ready to impersonate young love, Famous Players began to cast her as a child. It was an immediate and furious hit. A benevolent trick of nature had given her the ankles of a slim little girl. And mentally it was as though those hard early experiences had mixed up inextricably her childhood and maturity. Put her into pinafores and she was eight years old again. She stood and walked and ran and managed her head like a child; she even held her hands like a child. Presently, a French dramatic critic was calling her "the greatest ingénue in the world." *A Good Little Devil* and *Tess of the Storm Country*, wherein her shadow-self seems perhaps fifteen or sixteen, established her as a great star. Then Famous Players bought the film rights to Eleanor Gates's play *The Poor Little Rich Girl*. This production carried Mary Pickford's name and her shadow image even to the clearings by the African jungle, the atolls of the South Seas, the river settlements of China. It made her the most famous woman of her time. Its long success, both at home and abroad, pulled Famous Players past all financial danger and established it on the heights of security—so far as there is security in the moving-picture business.

Before that, however, Adolph Zukor was to totter again on the perilous verge of ruin. This crisis arose not from his own large and bold attitude toward the future, but from a blow of fate. Beginning as a tragedy, it ended perhaps as a comedy.

In those days, insurance companies looked on the inflammable film with great suspicion. The famous Charity Bazar fire in Paris, which started in a cinema booth, had accentuated that prejudice. Also, the business was so new that actuaries had not calculated the appropriate premiums. Insurance let the moving picture strictly alone.

Frank Meyer, realizing this, had at the very beginning looked into the matter of a fireproof safe for their precious negatives. He chose a huge affair, protected both with an asbestos lining and vacuum cells. When it arrived it seemed too heavy for a somewhat insecure floor already burdened with a tank. So he had it fastened to the wall by a pair of steel straps. Presently, the fire inspector, looking over this dangerous establishment, noted the arrangement and vetoed it on the spot. It imposed, he said, too much strain on that wall. Some day, wall and safe might come down together and crash through both floors onto the braid factory below. In the event of a fire, it would surely bring down the wall. Meyer, who is something of an engineer, did not believe him. And to move the film safe to another locality would entail innumerable inconveniences. He appealed to the fire commissioners. They had the matter under advisement, when the expected happened—also the unexpected.

On the night of September 11, 1915, Packy McFarland and Mike Gibbons fought in New York for the lightweight championship. The studio, from top to bottom, happened to be mad over boxing. Virtually everyone was going—except Frank Meyer. Mechanical superintendent of the firm, he served also as its filmcutter. Absorbed in a peculiarly intricate problem, he determined to work it out that night and gave away his ticket. As they passed out on their way to dinner, the studio force guyed his enslavement to duty. By half-past six the studio was empty except for a few mechanics working overtime on the lower floor, and Frank Meyer, cutting film on the upper. The safe stood open, and hundreds of thousands of dollars' worth of negatives and prints lay scattered over the shelves. Finally, one of the stage hands, an Italian, was visiting a friend in a flat just across the light-well.

The mechanics looked out of their window. They saw the Italian making wild, dramatic gestures. He was a bit of a clown; they took his performance for some of his characteristic monkeyshines and responded with derisive grimaces. He was trying, as a matter of fact, to give an alarm; he had seen that the braid factory below was a cauldron of flames. . . . Despairing of making them understand, he scrambled down the fire escape and up the one which led to their window. Even as he threw it open, the fire had burst the panes of the braid factory. As they jumped to the fire escape one of the mechanics remembered Frank Meyer and ran back. The fire was rushing up the stairway. He called; Meyer's voice answered. Remembering that a ladder ran from the cutting room to the roof, he leaped back to the fire escape and escaped just in time.

Meyer had sat so absorbed in his work that a choking sensation in his throat gave him the first warning; then the house fire alarm clanged from below. He thought first of the precious, fragile films. Gathering an armful, he ran to the stairway. It was afire. He rushed back to the safe, chucked into it haphazardly the films from his arms, from the table, from the racks. By the time he had closed the safe door he was choking with the thick smoke and the area by the staircase was burning like tinder. He scurried up the ladder, and butted his way through the hatchment. The tar roof was already afire from another quarter, and the opening of the hatchment had created a draught on which smoke and fire, fed now by raw film, shot up like a geyser. As he ran to the edge, the flames seemed to chase him across the roof. He dropped to the next building, and a jet of water from a hose drenched him to the skin. It was a chilly night and as he scrambled down the fire escape he decided to get a taxicab and go home for dry clothing. . . .

Meantime, Adolph Zukor, who himself intended to see the fight, was dining at the Knickerbocker Grill with the adolescent Eugene. Mr. and Mrs. Emil Shauer, who were going to the theatre, sat at another table. They finished, and strolled together out to the car. Traffic on Broadway had stopped, fire bells sounded from every direction, and a glow lit the southwestern sky.

"Quite a fire," remarked Zukor to a policeman at the curb.

"Yes," responded the policeman casually, "general alarm. It's a moving-picture studio on West Twenty-sixth Street."

When Frank Meyer returned in his dry clothes he had some difficulty in crashing through the police lines. Up and down between the engines strode Adolph Zukor, weeping frank, and open, and unashamed tears.

"He's taking his loss hard," thought Frank Meyer. "Well, he's got a licence." At that moment Zukor saw him, ran to him, embraced him, stood off feeling him all over and laughing hysterically with relief. For Frank Meyer was reported missing—when he went home to forefend pneumonia, he had not thought of that possibility. The last heard of him was his voice, calling to the mechanics across the blazing stairway.

All night the partners in this emperilled venture

stood inside of the police lines, watching the fire burn to its maximum and decline. That safe, steel-lashed to the wall, held the negatives of seventeen films; many of the most important still unprinted. If the wall fell in and dropped it into the superhot furnace below, fireproof safe or no fireproof safe, they were gone. And so, probably, was Famous Players—just as it was getting onto its feet. Those little rolls of celluloid represented all their product for six months; and they had not a cent of insurance. But the wall held; and toward morning they could see through the smoke the safe hanging aloft like a dovecote. Even then, they could not be sure.

The experts on fireproof safes, arriving next morning, seemed even less sure. Ordinary papers, they said, would resist the heat. But films, being mere celluloid, blazed and exploded at a comparatively low temperature. Had Frank Meyer, when he closed and locked the door, also thrown in the combination? That would make a great difference. Meyer cudgelled his brain, but he could not remember. Choking with smoke, in peril of his life, he had acted on instinct. They could not know until the safe cooled. That would take two or three days.

His associates remark yet on Zukor's calm during this crisis. That very morning he set to work as steadily, as systematically, as though this were a minor incident. He called the company together and assured them that their salaries would be paid on Saturday night as usual. He leased for a studio Durland's abandoned riding academy in Fifty-sixth Street. His competitors, expressing a fine tradition of American business, offered him a loan of all their spare facilities. He sped arrangements for resuming production at the earliest possible moment. His anxious associates wondered if he lacked imagination. In truth, he had too much imagination; he was shutting the door on it lest it overwhelm him. "I wouldn't let myself think that those films might be gone," he said afterward. "I was afraid I'd break down if I did." Even on the fateful morning when mechanics and firemen lowered the cooled safe from the wall and set it in place to open he remained in his temporary office, madly at work.

Frank Meyer laid a trembling hand on the lock. No, he had not thrown in the combination! He took a long breath, opened the doors.

Not even the edge of a film was scorched!

Tradition in the moving-picture business calls this the great crisis of the Famous Players. Zukor disagrees. The company was on its feet now, past the peak, a going concern. Even had these films burned, he believes that he would have fought through. The really dangerous crisis was that "low spot" of the summer before—the episode of Daniel Frohman's check.

This was his last flirtation with financial embarrassment. Henceforth, he struggled not against bankruptcy, but toward leadership and control and power.

BOOK III

FRUITION

CHAPTER XVI

AND NOW, HOLLYWOOD!

*N*ow we must go for a time far afield and begin life anew with Samuel Goldwyn, Jesse Lasky, and Cecil De Mille.

Goldwyn was born Goldfish. However, during his later adventures in moving pictures, he formed with Edgar Selwyn one of his characteristically brief partnerships; they combined their names and titled it the Goldwyn Company. The partnership broken, Goldfish kept the name for himself. I shall use it henceforth, even though I anticipate chronology. He sprang from Poland. During his infancy his family moved to Birmingham, England, and set up a small antique business. Expressing that independence, that lone-wolf quality, which has marked all his career, he ran away from home at the age of twelve, worked his passage to America, and found a job as apprentice in a glove factory at Gloversville, New York. He had scarcely perfected himself as a journeyman when he shifted to the business end of the industry and began selling gloves on the road. His aggressive energies brought early success; and before he was thirty he owned a glove agency in New York City. There he met Jesse Lasky.

The son of a merchant of San Jose, California, Lasky

had grown up expecting a course at Stanford University and a career in the law. His father's death ruined that. In his early teens he began carrying newspapers in Oakland, branched out to a small agency, and came into the old San Francisco *Post* first as clerk in the circulation department and afterward as reporter. When, near the turn of the century, the Cape Nome discovery blazed through the West, he rushed to Alaska. He found no gold; and, as John L. Sullivan once said in disgust of a wayward nephew, "he took to music"; for the cornet had fascinated him from infancy. Next, he was in Honolulu, the only white man in the Royal Hawaiian Band. Returning to San Francisco, he found that his sister Blanche had grown proficient with the cornet. They formed a team—"The Musical Laskys"—and toured for a season or so on the local Orpheum circuit. An Eastern manager offered them an engagement at one hundred dollars a week. They came East, bringing their mother, and "opened" in Boston.

Flat disappointment followed. Their act, said the manager, was not up to "the big time." They saw that themselves, and dropped back to a small circuit at the old salary of fifty dollars a week, on which the three of of them managed somehow to exist for two or three years. Finally, the Musical Laskys found themselves the vaudeville relief to Herman the Magician. This company carried a treasurer, who stood watch at the door over the local ticket taker. Somewhere in Pennsylvania the incumbent quit his job. Jesse Lasky, whose act did not begin until half-past nine, thereupon "doubled" in the box office. This service brought him the acquaintance of advance agents, local managers, and theatre owners; he became interested in vaudeville as a business. By now he realized that he would never climb Parnassan heights as a cornet player. He saw an opening toward affluence—devising and managing "musical acts." In an interior New York town he had met B. A. Rolfe, a cornettist with a thrill in every note. Some call him the greatest trumpeter in the world. Lasky sketched out an act for him, and booked it tentatively. An offer of fifty per cent. more than his salary as orchestra leader drew Rolfe to the footlights. Eventually he and Lasky formed a partnership, and sprinkled the Eastern circuits with musical acts. Lasky originated the business and sketched the rough plots for turns comic, turns serious, turns beautiful. He dressed his bijou bands in rich uniforms and labelled them the "Colonial Sextette" or the "Military Octette." He found ways of torturing music out of stage furniture. He hammered jokes and bits of business, purchased at two dollars apiece from professional "gag men," into knockout vaudeville acts. The vaudeville mania was rising toward its peak and he prospered astonishingly. Growing ambitious, he started with the Harris firm the "Folies Bergère," the first cabaret in New York. This opened, in an artificially cooled theatre, during the summer of

1911. Through various causes, including a hot wave and the ineptitude of theatrical men at restaurant keeping, it failed dismally. Very much behind the game now, Lasky went back to his vaudeville turns.

He found room on a major circuit for a comic opera complete in one act. Having a composer already in mind, he thought of William De Mille as librettist. Mrs. Henry De Mille, mother of William, managed the business affairs of her artistic sons. Lasky saw her. No, William could not trifle with vaudeville, said Mrs. De Mille. His play, *The Woman*, with Jane Peyton, had scored a major hit, and orders for other dramas were piling up. But her younger son, Cecil, had given up his job as a stage director and taken to playwriting. He had, Mrs. DeMille felt, a better comedy touch than William. Lasky struck a bargain for Cecil. The opera proved more than satisfactory, and Cecil booked with Lasky and Rolfe several other one-act sketches at the conventional royalty of twenty-five dollars a week.

Meantime, the restless Goldwyn had become enamoured of the screen. In the summer of 1913, when Zukor had just opened a way for the long film, Arthur Friend, a theatrical lawyer, called his attention to its possibilities. Returned from his vacation, Goldwyn ranged the town, entering every motion-picture house he passed. During that vital season of new enterprises, there appeared in New York *The Delhi Durbar*, a glorified news-feature seven reels long, which for the first time ambitiously introduced colour into the film. Goldwyn went mad over it. He began hammering at Lasky. "My business experience and your theatrical experience —look at it!" he said.

Lasky was in no mood for adventure. However, as he sat one night that autumn at dinner with Cecil De Mille, they floated into a mood of pessimism. "Here I am, back where I started," said Lasky.

"And here I am, just writing cheap vaudeville turns," said De Mille.

Suddenly, something which he cannot quite explain even yet happened in Lasky's mind. He had made the leap!

"Cecil," he said, "let's go into the moving-picture business!"

"Now Cecil," said Lasky afterward, "was this sort of a fellow in those days: if I'd proposed something sensible, he'd have turned it down cold, but if I'd proposed to start a filibustering expedition to Thibet, he'd have bit like a fish. He answered 'Why not?'"

Threshing out the details, they strolled over to The Lambs, the great exchange for theatrical ideas. There in the taproom sat Dustin Farnum. He had starred on the road all the past season in Edwin Milton Royle's huge success, *The Squaw Man*. Also, he had occupied his vacation in touring Europe with Walter Hale while they filmed C. N. & A. M. Williamson's *The Lightning Conductor*. Both Lasky and De Mille knew this.

"Let's start with Dusty Farnum in *The Squaw Man*," said De Mille.

"All set," responded Lasky.

In such offhand manner began the Lasky Feature Play Company! Two days of close conference, and they had perfected their organization, thrown together their programme. Lasky, the skilled and well-known manager of the group, was to be president and give his name to the corporation. Lasky and De Mille subscribed each to $5,000 worth of stock in a $26,500 capitalization. Goldwyn took most of the rest. Farnum agreed to accept $5,000 worth of stock for his services. On second thought, he changed his mind. He was an actor, he said, not a business man. Instead of shares, he would take a salary. That stock which he refused has grown through successive combinations and divisions to a value of more than a million dollars. Yet no one can call Farnum foolish to choose as he did. In sober truth, a whirl at business is usually a disaster for any artist. And at that period, moving pictures had the same standing with the stock market as dry oil wells or unplanted rubber plantations. But, "opportunity knocked at my door, and I wasn't in," says Farnum.

Royle sold them picture rights to *The Squaw Man* for ten thousand dollars, mostly notes. This was nearly two fifths of their capital; and long pictures had begun to cost money. Winter was coming on, and they had determined to produce it in the Southwest, so transportation added another expense. Further, they must buy all the initial equipment of a studio. But in Goldwyn they had a dynamic super-salesman. While De Mille, Farnum, and a scratch-up company started West, Goldwyn and Lasky remained in New York, selling the non-existent picture to independent states' rights buyers for cash or for notes which they might discount at the bank.

For a location, they had selected Los Angeles. It lay close to Wild Western scenery; its heterogeneous population would furnish cowboys and Indians for extra people; and there was the celebrated climate. Already, moving-picture people had used that region for winter operations; notably Griffith and Mary Pickford two years before. As an alternative, they considered Flagstaff, Arizona, which none of them had ever seen but whose name on the map attracted them. De Mille and Farnum started with instructions to look over Flagstaff on the way. They viewed it from the car window, found it unpromising for cinema purposes, and went on to Los Angeles.

In the orange-growing suburb of Hollywood they found a barn which another moving-picture company had revamped the winter before as a studio. They rented it for a hundred dollars a week, and paid extra for the privilege of digging up some unconveniently placed orange trees. Life in Hollywood was then extremely primitive. The town had no tram cars and the Lasky

Company owned as yet only one piece of mechanical transportation—a second-hand truck which served to haul scenery, property, and actors alike. When they worked "on the lot" they walked a mile to their very humble boarding houses; "on location" they camped out. De Mille, coached by screen-wise members of the company and by his mechanics, started at the same time to produce a super-film and to learn a new trade. Goldwyn was shrieking over the wire for speed, speed, and yet more speed. In two or three hectic weeks De Mille finished. They rushed the negative to print, projected it.

Something was wrong. The film ran jerkily, haltingly, insanely. Mechanics overhauled the apparatus, and found the trouble. It looked irreparable.

Everyone must have noticed, in printed reproduction of films, the regular perforations which run to both sides of the picture. The cogs of both cameras and projectors, fitting into these holes, produce the swift dance of the film past the lens. Already, the process was standardized; all American equipment demanded sixty-four perforations to the foot. Mysteriously, the new film which they brought to Los Angeles had sixty-five perforations to the foot. It worked all right in the camera; the famous "Latham loop," designed to take up slack, attended to that. But the film-printing machine reproduces on the positive both the pictures and the perforations of the negative. And in the less elastic projector that extra perforation played singular pranks. The picture was spoiled. They had produced it largely from money advanced by the distributors. This meant ruin. . . .

Their mechanics tried to patch it up and merely spoiled the negative. Then, when all seemed lost, De Mille uncovered his buried ace. He is a creature of instincts and intuitions. From the first, a vague worry over the negative had disturbed this able apprentice. That strip of frail celluloid held all their fortunes. It interpreted itself in his conscious mind as a fear of fire. "Luckily, I followed my hunch," says De Mille. To-day, the director "shoots" every scene four or five times, and from the "rough run" selects the one filming which shows the best results. In 1913, that refined method was virtually unknown. But De Mille cannily filmed every scene twice, and stored the extra negative in his boarding-house room. Now, they took no more chances with their own mechanics. They carried De Mille's hidden treasure straight to Lubin of Philadelphia, the most expert film doctor in the trade. In consideration of a contract for making the prints, he put his ingenuity to work and solved the problem. Breathing freely again, De Mille swung into a film version of George Barr McCutcheon's *Brewster's Millions*, which Lasky had bought for its next production.

Sales of *The Squaw Man* returned to the Lasky Company almost twice the cash value of their original capital.

Owing to the necessity for speed, Lasky and Goldwyn had slung it forth without much preliminary advertising and ballyhoo. Having this time more leisure, they followed the example set for his business by Zukor, and gave *Brewster's Millions* a promotional showing in New York. For publicity reasons, they herded into the theatre every stage and screen notability that friendship or favour could cajole. Among them came Adolph Zukor. Next morning he telephoned congratulations to Lasky; the day after, invited him to luncheon. Lasky was flattered; and this is a measure of Zukor's sudden rise. Less than two years before, theatrical Broadway knew him not, and moving-picture Broadway only as a small exhibitor with hallucinations about the future of the business. Now, an invitation from him was a guerdon, a decoration!

However, Zukor sought Lasky's acquaintance not merely by way of pleasing a young aspirant. He had been watching his competitors, as he always does. With his special faculty for putting his personality and desires out of the problem, he had searched their product not for his own flattering reassurance but to establish its points of superiority—and to learn. He had liked *The Squaw Man*, and *Brewster's Millions* pleased him even better. Lasky, De Mille, and Goldwyn, indeed, formed an exceptional combination. Goldwyn brought to the film, besides his business talent and his power of salesmanship, a primal love of a story and an instinctive understanding of the screen. De Mille possessed an inherited feeling for dramatic values, a keen sense of beauty, and fertility of large if vague ideas. Lasky, like Zukor an adventurer with life and already a trained showman, was fast developing what the writers in his employ call "his editorial faculty." He glows to other people's ideas; knows how to expand them, make them practicable. Also, he is an unsurpassed discoverer of screen talent. And all three had the priceless gift of invention.

Meeting across a luncheon table at Delmonico's, Zukor and Lasky found that their minds dovetailed, and that they had similar aims. Zukor summed that all up in one of the commercial phrases which he carried over from the fur business into art—"a high-class product, and nothing else."

Whenever Lasky flashed into town from Hollywood where his company was producing to the limit of its borrowing capacity, they met at luncheon to discuss the larger strategies of the moving-picture business. They found that the movement of the times was edging them into coöperation. The states' rights system, by which they had distributed their first pictures, was no longer adequate to their uses. The best exhibitors, as I have said already, were demanding a continuous supply of those new-fangled, six-reel, super-star films. The two-reelers—with Chaplin always the brilliant exception—were fading back into the slum houses. In a combination, Zukor, Lasky, and the new, promising California firm of Bosworth, could by crowding all steam put out 104 pictures a year—two a week. They needed only to unite behind some new combination of distributors. The Trust, distribution system and all, was fast disintegrating. Out of the wreckage, new combinations were taking form. One of these—Paramount—Zukor took pains to hurry along. Presently, Paramount was sending forth a Famous Players-Lasky-Bosworth programme of the desired 104 pictures a year. Of these, Famous Players furnished fifty, Lasky thirty, Bosworth ten, leaving the other fourteen to be picked up from the small but ambitious companies now overrunning all California. Fifty "big" pictures a year strained for the time Zukor's resources for raising money. But, to keep in the lead, he must expand.

That is the plain, statistical statement of a business arrangement which involved much drama, much clash of ruthless, dominant characters. Here, I shall take a new breath and go back again into the past.

Jesse L. Lasky

Airplane view of Paramount Famous Lasky Corporation's studio in Hollywood

CHAPTER XVII

A DUEL

OUT of the West came W. W. Hodkinson, another man of small beginnings who, scanning the world from little store shows in Poverty Hollow, had visioned moving-picture palaces in the heart of Main Street. When moving-picture journalism was still merely a weapon of the war between trust and independents, he contributed to his favourite weekly a speculative and imaginative article on the future of the business. It stood, he said, at the beginning of great things. Before long the price at the door would rise from five cents to ten and finally to twenty-five. Then would come the long film, a whole evening's entertainment on the scale and dignity of a dramatic performance. After which the film would begin taking over the regular theatres and charging theatrical prices. The moving-picture business read, and smiled. It was interesting, but also touching and fantastic. Of course, the reality exceeded Hodkinson's wild flight of imagination. But before 1911 or 1912 probably only two men of any consequence saw the outcroppings of a bonanza—the little, quiet, subtle Hungarian Jew in South Union Square and the tall, hustling, high-powered Yankee in Utah.

For it was in Utah that Hodkinson entered the moving-picture business—stumbled into it, as did most of the pioneers. He was in 1907 a salesman for the correspondence school which had given him most of his business education, and growing a little weary of the job. The movies arrived in Ogden. Probably, in that early day and remote region, they represented the worst of the primitive one-reelers—lynchings, with the victim strung up in full view of the audience, realistic murders, a shocking display of the female ankle. The better element was talking of censorship. Full of uplifting educational ideals, Hodkinson conceived a family theatre running films at which propriety need not blush. He raised a little capital in Ogden, secured moral backing from the newspapers, and hung out his sign. He was perhaps the first exhibitor to charge ten cents instead of five; and at that price, he made his theatre pay.

He is by temperament a business man, as Zukor is perhaps primarily an artist. Creation of films never attracted him. He passed from exhibition to distribution and acquired an agency of his own for the Pacific Coast. When the Trust formed the General Film Company, he sold out to the combination and became its manager for the coast and the intermountain region. Even with the unsatisfactory films the New York companies gave him, he managed through his energy and personal influence to raise all standards in his territory—better theatres, higher prices, superior trimmings of orchestras and decorations. While in the East moving pictures lay still under ban of the respectable, in his territory they began to advance toward Main Street. He was the star of the General Film Company, the bright example of conventions and conferences. Also, he had acquired some money of his own and much standing with the banks.

When the current of the times cracked the Trust and the government decisions began to hammer it into fragments, Hodkinson formed a distributing company of his own; in a year or so he outstripped his competitors of the Pacific Coast. All over the country, the same thing was happening; the fragments of the Trust were combining into larger companies. W. L. Sherry had begun to dominate the important New York territory. Abrams and Greene virtually controlled distribution in New England; and so on.

In January, 1914, and at about the time when Zukor and Lasky had begun acutely to worry over the lack of a stable and regular outlet, Hodkinson came East and solicited from Zukor, already the most important of the "high-class" producers, the contract to distribute Famous Players films. There followed negotiations too complex to narrate in detail. Zukor wanted from the first to throw Lasky into the bargain. Hodkinson, however, is another man who thinks "three years ahead." Half-consciously he seems to have perceived the force and ambition underlying the quiet surface of Adolph

Zukor, and to have exaggerated a danger, as men of lively imagination will. The Trust, by monopolizing production, had strangled progress. The Famous Players, embodied in Zukor, then led the field in production of first-class films, and Lasky stood next in merit. Perhaps they, too, were working toward a monopoly! Also, one suspects, these two dominant temperaments clashed. Hodkinson wanted the Lasky pictures, but separately and on his own terms.

Zukor was not looking toward monopoly of production; his need at the moment was a large and regular outlet. Machinery there was, scrapped from wreckage of the Trust, to distribute short films. The makers of super-films, like him and Lasky, must still depend on the uncertain states' rights system. What they wanted was a smooth and certain machine throwing out to distributors two changes of programme a week. Using Mary Pickford's popular *Tess of the Storm Country* as a lever, he had Al Lichtmann call the chief executives of the big distributing firms to New York. They represented five groups, strong enough to cover with sub-agents and agencies the whole United States. And, as a resolution of strangely warring forces, they pooled their interests in the Paramount Picture Corporation, with W. W. Hodkinson president and general manager. The Zukor, Lasky, and Bosworth companies accepted it as distributing agency, and perfected the two-film-a-week arrangement which I described in the last chapter.

Paramount was to receive thirty-five per cent. of the gross receipts from sale of films to the moving-picture theatres; the producers, sixty-five per cent. The adversaries, now temporary allies, both profited by the arrangement. Hodkinson, from a local agent, had sprung to rule of a company which distributed nation-wide the best moving pictures then current; Zukor had found a perfect outlet.

However, both men, and especially Zukor, regarded the arrangement as a truce, not a peace. The president of the Famous Players had been looking ahead. He also entertained fears and suspicions, born from memories of the Trust. At the end of his long vision loomed a vague peril. If the brilliant, energetic Hodkinson went ahead he might gather the sales agencies for all the long-film companies under the roof of Paramount. A combination of these middlemen could hold the bridge between the producer and the ultimate consumer, taking toll. Again, as under the Trust, men who did not understand might strangle progress. In a great crisis, such as the "low spot" of 1913, the fire of 1915, Zukor goes deathly still—"the one quiet amidst the raging floods." In face of a far-away perplexity like this, he comes out of his shell and grows almost voluble. He used to drag Sam Goldwyn, the business executive of the Lasky Company, on long walks, and while wearing him out with his own swift, steady gait of a trapper, review the same situation in the same words. And, as a matter of fact, the equally resolute and ambitious Hodkinson was blazing exploratory trails toward new horizons. All this time, gossips and go-betweens were fanning up the resentments of these born antagonists.

During the two years of the temporary arrangement between the producers and Paramount, there arose new problems which made the future seem to Zukor even more clouded. The great moving-picture boom, of which later I shall treat in more detail, was rising toward its climax. Stars—and rightly, considering their drawing power—were beginning to demand salaries beyond the dreams of bank presidents. Zukor was paying Mary Pickford a thousand dollars a week, then two thousand, then—but I will save the last figure for a climax. *Zenda*, his original production of 1912, cost $7,000. By 1915 or 1916, a rather ordinary film might cost $40,000. The "million-dollar film" was on its way. As the expense of production mounted, the producer must pay from his sixty-five per cent. of gross receipts the interest on increased investment; while the distributor, running along on the same old scale, got his thirty-five per cent. just the same.

Also, the project known as First National was a-borning. It said to stars, directors, and actors: "Our company will produce and also distribute. Why pay a middleman's profit?" Eventually, if not immediately, he must meet this kind of competition.

The existing contracts between Paramount and the three producing firms were due soon to expire. Disquieting rumours of Hodkinson's intentions reached Zukor and Lasky. First—Paramount, said the gossips, was flirting with the American Tobacco Company. That corporation had of late reached far afield, gathering up and financing enterprises which had nothing to do with Havana fillers or Connecticut leaf. Zukor and Lasky felt out a certain roving executive of the tobacco company. He talked of a combination, financed by his corporation, between Famous Players, Lasky, the Triangle Company of Chicago and Hollywood, and Paramount; and talked in such manner as to suggest an understanding with Hodkinson. Once, Goldwyn met him in the offices of Paramount. "And he had," said Goldwyn a decade later, "the air of owning the place. Only a bluff maybe—but it was disquieting." Zukor and Hodkinson were keeping suspiciously away from each other.

Yet Paramount was the only system of distribution then available for Zukor's large purpose. Looking over the fields, he saw a possible avenue of escape—that same Triangle Company which Tobacco had suggested as a partner. "In those days," says a veteran executive of Famous Players, "some competitor or other was forever pounding at our heels. Often, he even passed us on the turns." The dangerous contender in 1916 was Triangle. Formed and expanded by a bewildering combination and recombination of several old companies, it had acquired Griffith, high in the glory of his epoch-

making *Birth of a Nation*, had started Douglas Fairbanks on his career, had gathered under its studio roof
such leading actors of stage and screen as Willie Collier,
De Wolf Hopper, Raymond Hitchcock, Billie Burke,
Julia Dean, and that new king of the Westerns, W. S.
Hart. It was creating its own system of distribution.
Pile a-top Famous Players and Lasky this important
firm, and you had a structure so commanding that it
could, as it chose, dictate to Paramount or create its own
distribution. Soon Harry E. Aitken, president of Triangle, sat in conference with Famous Players and Lasky.

The negotiations which followed involved so many
factors and so many plans as to blur the memories of
the high contracting parties; the course of events remains to this day a little obscure. At one period a banking syndicate, which wanted to take over the whole
project, offered Zukor $1,500,000 for his interest in
Famous Players. Though security for his family tempted
him who had known poverty and insecurity, power and
activity tempted him even more. He declined. Again,
Triangle and the "Paramount firms" reached the point
of drawing up a tentative agreement. Then someone in
the Famous Players forces discovered that Triangle
wanted virtually to reserve its foreign rights. This
source of revenue had become important; must become
in the future, Zukor and Goldwyn saw, more important
still. The agreement went into the waste-paper basket;

and while negotiations were not broken off, the project dozed.

But gossip floated somehow through the cracks of the conference rooms. The Hotel Astor was then stamping ground for executives of the motion-picture business. Through its lobbies and cafés, men passed the rumour in whispers which increased to shouts. And at this moment Zukor took a vacation. He was weary to the point of collapse. The old itching again disturbed his skin. He retired to French Lick Springs, leaving his whereabouts a mystery to everyone except the inside circle of his offices. The said inside circle had dinner and luncheon every day at the Astor. When gossip, putting two and two together, said that Zukor was really in Chicago signing up with Triangle, the central group of Famous Players only smiled significantly and mysteriously.

Into the Astor came the directors of Paramount, representing five groups of stockholders. They heard the gossip. That season Hodkinson had perhaps pulled a little away from the majority of his company. Like Zukor, he was "always in a hurry." He had been talking expansion, eventual control. The rest were contented with the very profitable present arrangement and desired not to risk any loss of the Zukor-Lasky contract. If, now, Zukor was flirting with Triangle . . . There were tentative meetings across luncheon tables at the Astor, and then conferences behind locked doors and stuffed keyholes. Suddenly Zukor, summoned by telegraph, returned from French Lick.

On June 13, 1916, Hodkinson called to order in his office the annual meeting of the Paramount Company. Financially, he had a good year to report. In recognition of his record and his ability, Paramount had elected him its original president, and had reëlected him in 1915; no reason to suppose that the directors wanted a change. Hodkinson entertained a motion that they dispense with minutes.

"The next in order is nomination of offices for the ensuing year," he said perfunctorily.

Hiram Abrams rose from his seat in the corner.

"I nominate——" he began. And then an overwhelming sense of the drama in the situation fairly choked him. "I nominate——" he repeated, and choked again. When again he enacted this odd performance, the suppressed nerves of Walter Greene, his partner, burst through into action.

"I nominate Hiram Abrams for president," he called.

Before Hodkinson came out of his trance it was all over. By a vote of three to two Paramount had elected Hiram Abrams president. Hodkinson asked no questions; the act spoke for itself. In the mood of steely quiet which disaster casts over the Anglo-Saxon, he put on his hat without a word, and walked from the room.

Abrams took the chair.

"On behalf of Adolph Zukor, who has purchased my

shares in Paramount, I call this meeting to order," he said.

Production had taken the reins from distribution; Zukor had won. Hodkinson continued in the motion-picture business, and achieved success and a fortune with other enterprises. But, except for the negotiations preceding sale of his stock, he had no further commerce with Paramount.

In the next few months, Adolph Zukor sprinkled scare-heads over all the motion-picture trade journals; he even broke into the front pages of the secular newspapers. Two weeks after Paramount elected Abrams president, he announced the amalgamation of Famous Players, the Lasky Feature Play Company and Bosworth, together with a few smaller companies which had been distributing their product through Paramount. All this time, circumstances had forced Zukor and Lasky into closer and closer coöperation. Their interests had become so nearly identical that it was only a step to that meeting at luncheon when Zukor remarked, suddenly and casually, "Why don't we combine?"

A decade later, Lasky said: "We weren't nearly so big as Famous Players at the time. I expected that he'd offer us a minor partnership, and that we'd settle down to traffic and bargain. I cleared my throat and asked, 'On what terms?' and Adolph answered casually, 'Oh, about fifty-fifty!' Adolph thinks so far and on such big terms that he never haggles over a thing like that. He prefers to have everyone contented—and then go ahead."

Zukor said: "I saw their product was better than mine and that if they stayed in competition, they might beat me. After all, the film's the thing."

Without argument, they made Zukor president and manager of finances and Jesse Lasky vice-president and manager of production; the arrangement endures to this day. Even this large company was too small, however, long to include four such able, positive characters as Zukor, Lasky, Goldwyn, and De Mille. In three months the restless Goldwyn had sold out to his partners. He formed with Edgar Selwyn the Goldwyn Company, merged that into the Metro-Goldwyn Company, again broke off all partnerships and began producing for himself. Five or six years later Cecil De Mille, who had concerned himself entirely with the creation and direction of big pictures, sold out his share and formed the De Mille Company.

Then Zukor made an announcement which gossips in the moving-picture business had long discounted. Famous Players-Lasky had bought Paramount. "A $25,000,000 merger," said the newspapers, exaggerating present values if not future prospects. Zukor controlled his product from the first turn of the raw film in his cameras to delivering at the stage door. More important to history, he established precedent for the whole business. Now all the great companies have their own distributing companies.

Between these two announcements came another; less important, really, but much more attractive to the newspapers. Adolph Zukor had agreed to pay Mary Pickford $10,000 a week as a mere advance against her share of the profits in her own pictures. So had Adolph Zukor's mad enterprise grown in four years!

CHAPTER XVIII

THE TIDE ROLLS ON

$\mathcal{F}$OUR years—as Terry Ramsaye says, "the term of a college course." In 1912, Adolph Zukor was a small exhibitor in Fourteenth Street and the obscure, unheeded Columbus of a fantastic idea. In 1916, he sat by right of merit at the head of a $25,000,000 combination. In 1912, he waited for three hours at the anteroom of the Trust in order that he might make a humble suggestion. In 1916, his world came to his door. It all happened so rapidly and yet so naturally that he could scarcely visualize it. That period in his life, as he tries now to piece the hurried events together, seems to him like one of those hot rallies in a fight when the adversary presses close and you strike and guard only on blind instinct. Major crisis had followed major crisis—the "low spot" in 1913, the fire in 1915, the struggle for control of distribution; and every week brought its minor perplexities with temperamental stars, insufficient funds, dangerous rivalries. All about him the business was growing like a mushroom, grouping and regrouping itself like a kaleidoscope. Out of this flux constantly bubbled some enterprise which might threaten not only his supremacy but his very existence.

In 1914, just when he was gaining a slippery foothold, Europe had gone to war. He must needs readjust all his relations with that foreign market now growing so important. At thirty-nine, when he bought the rights to *Queen Elizabeth*, Zukor had still that full head of jet-black hair which came to a widow's peak on his forehead; and his face retained so much of its youthful comeliness that he might have appeared as leading juvenile in one of his own films. When at forty-three he signed the agreement which took over the Paramount Company, his hair was thinning and whitening at the temples and his cheeks falling into weary masses.

The twenty-five millions with which the newspapers tagged the Famous Players-Lasky-Paramount merger measures the length and force of that tide whose crest Zukor was riding. In 1912, none would have offered such a sum, even in hypothetical money, for the whole moving-picture business of the United States. In 1916, the Zukor combination, while momentarily the largest in the field, represented only a small part of the "moving-picture interests." The two principles which Zukor laid down when he entered production—full-length film performances and exploitation of actors—had succeeded even beyond his own imagination. The public clamoured for the longer films, and granted Mary Pickford, W. S. Hart, Charlie Chaplin, a dozen others, frenzied idolatry without parallel in the history of the world. John Drew or Mrs. Fiske or Lillian Russell showed their personalities to not more than a thousand spectators a night. Mary Pickford was playing to millions every night; and popular enthusiasms seem to roll up in geometrical ratio to the number of adherents and converts. It was a craze no longer, but an appetite.

The European war, bursting in August, 1914, curiously intensified the appetite and confirmed the habit. During the two years of our hesitation it exercised a subconscious fascination on us all. The news reel, a European development, was bringing from European battlefields such glimpses as the censor allowed. Exhibitors varied even the long films with news reels. People who had never entered a moving-picture show before came now to see with their own eyes *soixante-quinze* batteries in action, German Infantry on the march, Italian Alpini scaling the precipices, the king reviewing his armies, the premier leaving Parliament House. They remained to watch the "feature"; and so acquired the habit. Also the suppressed spiritual excitement of America came to the surface in a mania for amusement. Though the "road" was yielding before the impact of the moving picture, the legitimate houses of Broadway never did better.

During this period the moving picture perfected its own education. "My single chance for immortality," said Sarah Bernhardt when she consented to act for the film. Alas, all that remains to America of *Queen Elizabeth* is one disintegrating print in the storehouse of the Paramount laboratories. Frank Meyer, now laboratory superintendent, ran it off for me in 1927; not for years before that had anyone unwound it from its metal reel. Many of the other early Zukor-Lasky successes have rotted or disappeared. But enough survive to serve as a study of the six-reel film in process of evolution.

The technicians had advanced further, when Zukor began producing, than the dramatic artists of the craft. Even the very earliest films show clear photography; in spots, beautiful photography. True, it is a little monotonous; many subtleties of light and shading have come in since. But it gave the director flexible language for a plain story. In other important particulars, the screen had not yet begun to attain its possibilities. As though hypnotized by the motto "Famous Players in Famous Plays," the directors generally filmed the whole scene, background and all, just as the spectator sees it on the speaking stage. The star actress has an "emotional bit" which absorbs for the moment all the attention of her audience. To-day, the director either makes this a "close-up", showing only face and bust, or at least brings the camera near enough to cut out everything but her figure. In that day, she was usually just a detail in a large scene. Never once does Bernhardt appear closely enough or exclusively enough to let us see clearly her magnificent, darting changes of expression. It is as though we viewed her through a veil or through the wrong end of the opera glasses.

American directors, when they began with long films, repeated the same mistake and added some of their own. Held down in the period of their education to one or two reels, obliged often on those stingy terms to reproduce a whole complicated novel such as *Lorna Doone* or *Camille*, they sacrificed everything to swift, packed action; and the habit persisted in the new, ampler era. *Tess of the Storm Country*, a film which carried the fame of Mary Pickford over the world, never gives even the star a real chance to impress her personality upon her audience. When she pleads, she rushes into the scene like the victim in a "chase" picture, throws herself abruptly on to her knees, delivers a set of whirlwind gestures, rushes out. So compressed and complicated is the action that none of the intelligent party with whom I witnessed this film could afterward make a synopsis. Its furious hit seems now a little inexplicable.

Passing over two years, we come to *David Harum* with W. H. Crane—as fine an actor on the screen as behind the footlights. Now the film is approximating modern technique of stage management. The director brings Crane's effective bits near to us, gives him a chance to impress upon us a quaint and lovable personality. The important points of the story are emphasized and developed with some leisure; the unimportant slurred over. No child in the audience can fail to understand what it is all about. Photography itself has taken a few steps forward; has learned to emphasize the important. *Tess of the Storm Country* in its original form—afterward Mary Pickford remade the whole thing—is archaic; *David Harum*, except for the long hobble skirts of the women, might have been filmed yesterday.

Credit for these improvements belongs not wholly or even chiefly to that Zukor-Lasky group whose fortunes I am following. A director or cameraman cannot copyright his tricks and devices any more than an author can copyright his peculiarities of style. As soon as they appear on the screen, rivals study them and adapt or imitate. Others, now that their shackles had fallen, had begun to experiment on a large scale. Griffith, while still with Biograph, produced in *Judith of Bethulia* the first of our grandiose scenic films. The pack coursed after him; companies began ranging the world for famous locations such as the canals of Venice, the Roman Forum, the country houses of England. . . . That expensive method also has grown archaic. Clever scenic artists now build from laths and "staff," in the corner of the lot, Romes or Venices or Constantinoples so realistic that natives, when they see the film, cannot tell the difference. Breaking loose from all management and scraping together the capital wherever he could find it, Griffith produced from Thomas Dixon Junior's *The Clansman* his twelve-reel masterpiece *The Birth of a Nation*. Released just after Europe went to war, it re-

vived in this country the animosities and controversies
of the Civil War. It cost perhaps $100,000—an un-
precedented sum—and it yielded millions. Out-of-the-
way houses are showing it yet, for it tells a story simply
and with a sure instinct for essential points. Thomas
Ince was beating his own way toward modern form.
Charlie Chaplin, becoming his own director, was finding
new possibilities. Douglas Fairbanks, creator as well as
actor, was climbing from the ruck. Fox had discovered
Theda Bara, who wrote "vamp" into the language.
These discoverers dragged to tinsel glory in their trail
such new stars as Mae Marsh, Norma Talmadge, Mary
Miles Minter, Lillian and Dorothy Gish.

The "serial craze," born of a newspaper circulation
war in Chicago, rose, blazed, and vanished. This film
fashion is now so very dead that it needs description.
A producer put forth a weekly series of multiple-reel
melodramas, tied together by a leading woman and an
insoluble mystery—as *The Perils of Pauline*, *The Adventures of Kathlyn*, or *The Million Dollar Mystery*.
Concurrently, a newspaper printed the "running story"
and offered a prize for the best solution of the mystery.
It ran its course in less than two years. Zukor, for one,
refused to be tempted by its glittering possibilities of
quick returns. "Our policy is high-class films," he said.
"Besides, it won't last." However, it gave directors a
large field in which to experiment, and served further
to educate the screen in technique.

Meantime, the moving picture had come definitely out of the back streets. At first in the second-class cities and then in the first-class, theatre after theatre closed scene lofts and dressing rooms, denied all booking to road companies, and revamped its interior for purposes of the screen. The more enterprising showmen were beginning to instal orchestras. Then, attacking the citadel of the enemy, the screen moved on to Broadway, even to Times Square, the heart thereof. Always by now the more pretentious films opened in some Broadway theatre, for the purpose of adding to its New York receipts the initial prestige of a New York run. The Triangle Company took over the Knickerbocker Theatre as an all-time moving-picture house. Marcus Loew had gone quietly forward these seven or eight years acquiring theatres all over the country, operating them in circuits on his formula "vaudeville and pictures at popular prices." Already he had a Times Square theatre. Now, he altered the formula to "pictures and vaudeville." Michell Mark built—on a scale considered very large in those days—the Strand, first New York playhouse designed from its inception for moving pictures. Zukor, Loew, Mark—all three passed through that little Penny Arcade which they considered at the time such an unlucky venture, but which proved the touchstone for their fortunes. Now "picture men," passing in and out of the Hotel Astor, could see all up and down the Great White Way the electric signs that flashed proclamation of their spectacular rise. The Astor was as a mining camp where the newly rich, in exalted bewilderment, bandy fortunes and chatter in millions. . . .

And three thousand miles away, Hollywood had advanced far along the road from its origin as a sleepy Western village dozing among orange groves to its bizarre destiny. Already it was coming to be the most famous town of its size in the world. Lasky with *The Squaw Man*, first long film produced in the West, and with his subsequent productions, had crystallized that. Doubtless in any event the business would have found its centre of production near Los Angeles. That region offers open winters, a maximum of sunny days, actinic light, infinite variety of scenery and architecture; and the Los Angeles Chamber of Commerce, in soliciting new industries, misses few tricks. But except for the accident of the rented barn, destiny might have struck some other suburb than Hollywood.

American production began, of course, in New York, the theatrical centre. By 1916, however, some of the greater companies were working exclusively in Hollywood or its sub-suburbs, Culver City and Universal City. For a long time, Famous Players-Lasky split its artistic forces. Zukor, when he began his series of combinations, was planning his great studio in Long Island City, twenty minutes by subway from Times Square. Completed, Famous Players-Lasky used it for nearly ten years. After 1916, however, the Hollywood studio under Lasky carried most of the production. There was then a good reason for this division. Long Island City lay close to Eastern and European "locations." When, for example, Waldemar Young put Hergesheimer's *Java Head* into screen form, George Melford, the director, took his whole company to old Salem, setting of the novel. To-day—as I have said before—the studio scene painters build their locations on the lots. In two weeks they would construct on a half acre all the old Salem they needed for their purposes.

Further, New York's heterogeneous millions furnished a supply of unusual types, forms, and faces for special bits. But the beautiful and odd, the vain and ambitious, crowded so fast into Hollywood that soon every imaginable type stood registered in the books of the casting director. "If you want in a hurry a cross-eyed Lithuanian waiter who can act," said Lasky once, "or a dyspeptic, one-armed Arab, you may have to search for some time in New York. But in Hollywood— you can have him on the lot that afternoon." In 1926— to go far ahead of the story—Zukor and Lasky closed the Long Island studio, and concentrated all the studios at Hollywood. Others preceded or followed this movement; to-day, not a single first-class company produces habitually in the East. Yet from its towers of Times Square, New York governs the finances of the business, carries on most of its distribution, opens and exploits all its more pretentious creations. In no other American industry do management and distribution lie so far apart from production—three thousand miles of distance, four days by the fastest train. This could not be if the goods which the moving-picture companies make and sell were bulky. But one man can easily carry a set of negatives representing an expense of from $200,000 to $500,000; and in a pinch the studios send their unprinted films from Los Angeles to New York by air mail.

CHAPTER XIX

A CONQUEST OF WORLDS

I HAVE mentioned the European war casually, as though it were an episode only faintly pertinent to this subject. In fact, it affected profoundly not only Adolph Zukor's enterprises but all that bizarre business which he was leading toward the status of a major industry.

Even in the primitive age when the screen presented only scenery, street episodes, and trick effects of photography, producers trafficked back and forth across the Atlantic. We witnessed in New York the waves breaking on the chalk cliffs of Dover; London saw our fire department in action. Apace with us the Europeans, and especially the French, passed from scenes and tricks to stories. During the first decade of the century French films, by all artistic standards, excelled ours. I have told how, flaunting our superstitions, the French dared in 1911 to produce the four-reeler *Queen Elizabeth*. Nor did they hesitate to exploit their actors. Max Linder, under no curse of anonymity, anticipated Charlie Chaplin as an artistic comedian. Presently, British, Italians, and Germans were producing for the market. Indeed the Italians, taking advantage of their history and their historic backgrounds, advanced to the full-length

Cabiria and *Quo Vadis*, films which no one has as yet exceeded for scenic beauty.

No comparative statistics of early exports and imports survive. It seems likely that European films had for a time the favourable balance of trade. Then came our "Westerns." In old days the American Wild West dime novel enjoyed a great vogue in Europe. Melodrama was its essence; and simple souls love that. To the routine-bound European townsman and peasant it carried news of a wild, free atmosphere "where men are men." The Western films played on the same tastes. They were a furious hit, especially on the Continent. During the first stages of the European catastrophe, the French built in Paris their "Panthéon de la Guerre." Panels distributed through this panorama portrayed the leading statesmen and generals of the Allies, with representatives of the people in their national costumes and plying their typical tasks. When we entered the war, the French painted a panel for us. A group of cowboys in chaps and of Indians in war bonnets represented —exclusively—the American populace. The Western film stood responsible for that!

Presently, the balance of trade swung decisively our way. In the days of the Trust, such pioneers as Blackton saw the opportunity abroad, and worked to extend and to solidify the European market. As the Trust disintegrated, our foreign distribution passed into a period of confusion, though sales went steadily ahead. When toward the end of 1912 Zukor set the fashion for the long film, European distribution had settled down to a condition resembling our old states' rights system. A dealer in films either acted as agent for the American producer, or bought for a lump sum the right to distribute in his country.

Zukor placed his early films in the hands of a London agency. *The Prisoner of Zenda* sold well; and Mary Pickford's first long films brought from Great Britain, the Colonies, and the Continent very solid returns. Early in his operations, Zukor appointed Emil Shauer foreign manager. As a department-store buyer Shauer had learned his Europe; and as a showman, his films. In 1914, when the Powers were growling and mobilizing, Zukor found in the Paramount Company a secure and ample channel of distribution on a large scale. In 1916, while the German batteries still poured horror on Verdun, he soldered Paramount to his own machine. As others fell in and followed this type of organization, the inter-firm competition of America extended itself to Europe, and from there to remoter lands.

A remarkable and important coincidence, this. Just when the American moving picture bounded ahead of its European competitors, just when it perfected its business machinery, a blight fell upon Europe. Mobilization closed the studios of France, then of England, finally of Italy. . . . Late in 1917, I saw a small company of women and elderly men acting before the camera in a hotel lobby at Marseilles; and it looked like the last gasp. In this respect as in others Britain tried to maintain "business as usual," but before 1918 she gave up the struggle. Italy stayed with the game a little longer, and even in the heart of war made out of a gigantic actor who tossed oxen over the shoulder and carried a six-inch gun up the mountains with the Alpini, something of a star. But before the Armistice, she, too, was virtually out of the game. And this low curve of the European business coincided exactly with our greatest period of expansion.

Yet Europeans, even more than Americans, were gone mad for amusement—anything to make them laugh, make them forget, carry them out of themselves. The war blighted the spoken theatre, an unessential industry. The male actors and craftsmen were mostly of military age; they had rushed, or had been drafted, into the ranks. By 1917 the few anæmic reviews still showing in London got along with all-girl choruses and with crippled demobilized leading men. Into this vacuum poured the flood of American films. Mary Pickford's sunny curls, Mae Marsh's girlish innocence, and Theda Bara's sinister allure sweetened the war for millions of young and impressionable soldiers. Charlie Chaplin threw all Europe into hysterical war-laughter. I saw company-comedians imitating him in the trenches. As with America, so with Europe; the moving picture came out of the back streets. "Cinema houses" thrust into the environs of Trafalgar Square, into the Boulevards, the Corso, Unter den Linden. And more and more as the European supply fell away and as ours improved, they showed American films.

Even after we declared war, the American motion picture raced madly onward. At times, volunteering and the draft disorganized both Hollywood studios and New York offices. But the war weighed upon us rather lightly; and always other human material flowed at once into the vacuum. We concentrated four million young men into camps; they must needs be entertained and kept out of mischief of nights. The simple, portable moving picture solved this military problem. Our four million young soldiers had to watch moving pictures, whether they wished or no. This served further to confirm the habit with all classes of Americans.

When, the war finished, the Europeans tried to struggle back into production, it seemed as though they had fallen twenty years behind the times. The great American companies had by now perfected their system of foreign distribution and were cultivating the field intensively. The more ambitious films were all produced with an eye to the export market. In Hollywood or New York, specialists on foreign races edited and cut export films to fit the tastes, prejudices, and government regulations of fifty nations. For example: the English-speaking peoples like a happy ending. The Germans prefer an unhappy ending; the gloomier the better.

The Latins dislike to see the logically unhappy outcome of a situation twisted illogically to bring the scattered family together, the hero and heroine into each other's arms. It clashes with their inborn sense of form and art. So almost from the birth of the foreign trade in long films, producers were making two endings—one for the United States, Great Britain, and the Colonies, another for Continental Europe, South America, and the Orient. Foreign importers and jobbers of American goods used to complain that our manufacturers refused concessions to the tastes and wants of alien races. Had leadership in our motion-picture business remained with the old stock, Hollywood might have made the same general mistake. But Zukor, and all the men who followed him into larger fields, were either born in Europe or only one generation removed from its soil. They had the international mind.

When the world ceased firing, American films were travelling by every conveyance from aëroplane to llama-back into the atolls of the South Pacific, the highlands of the Andes, the jungles of Africa, and—of course—even the smallest hamlet of western Europe. How widely the trade has spread stands illustrated by one scene in De Mille's *The King of Kings*. The Christ stoops and writes in the sand with His finger. The inscription was part of the film itself; it could not be replaced with a translated title. So the director had this scene photographed twenty-eight times for twenty-eight languages ranging from French and English to Arabic and Chinese!

Before the European producer summoned energy and capital to compete with us, foreign audiences were growing accustomed to American scenes and ways— thinking of the screen in American terms. Also, as France, England, and Germany began to organize for production, they encountered a special commercial obstacle. Under stress of competition, the greater American producers were narrowing the margin between receipts and expenditures. Presently, they had so arranged things that they merely "broke even" on the domestic sales, and looked to the foreign market for profit. A European, building toward world-wide distribution, faced a hopeless, desperate situation. No other country in the world had so much as a quarter of our revenue from the domestic exhibition of a picture. We could make a "million-dollar film" pay for itself at home. The foreign producer, on the same terms, could afford to lay out no more than from $200,000 to $250,000. He could not naturally pay his actors or directors the inflated prices of Hollywood. As soon as a foreign star like Pola Negri or Emil Jannings rose high in the heavens, Hollywood prices drew him or her to California. Almost unchecked by native production, the American moving picture swept on to conquest of every country in the world. From eighty-five to ninety per cent. of the films shown abroad came from the United States. This in face of frantic official efforts to encourage European production and by propaganda, censorship, and even embargo, to discourage American imports.

Yet even if Europe had met us, during the period when the motion picture was finding itself, in equal and unfettered competition, we might have swept the world just the same. Probably they would have created pictures more acceptable to critical taste; but this narrative concerns itself with the motion picture as an industry, not as an art. The modern American stock, with its romantic background and its mixed origins, has positive qualities which equip it for this very job.

To begin with, Heaven endowed us above any other peoples with a developed narrative sense. We are story tellers. The peasants and wood cutters in the cafés of France and Belgium or Germany talk politics, primitive philosophy, even music and art. Northwestern lumbermen smoking in the shack after supper, Arizona cowboys squatting round the camp fire, fishermen mending their nets on the Gloucester wharves, tell racy anecdotes of self-experienced or vicarious adventure. The short story is our one first-class achievement in literature. We put this faculty into our films. Assisted by the imaginative Russians, the Germans have of late produced motion pictures excelling ours in sheer art. The sophisticated and the critical rave over *Dr. Calagari's Cabinet* and *The Last Laugh:* but the populace remains calm. In these great films, and even more in the ordinary product of German, French, and British studios, there is one common flaw. The story limps. It seems confused, illogical, ineffectively told. And the average European spectator—in fact, all the world of common folk—loves a story; demands subconsciously, even as children do, that it shall "hang together."

However, personality is the best-selling piece of goods in the theatrical manager's pack. In four cases out of five, the humble auditor or spectator does not carry away any specially vivid memory of that story which bases and frames the whole structure. He remembers only the flashing gorm of Douglas Fairbanks plying a rapier, the soft expressiveness of Rudolph Valentino making love, the refined charm of Florence Vidor, the alluring, restrained emotionalism of Lillian Gish. If the story halts or falters, he analyzes the defect only so far as to remark, "Fairbanks wasn't very good in this film."

And here, according to the majority of analytical managers, America has its best hold. As Lasky says, "Other peoples may hate America as America, but no one actively dislikes the American type." Even when solid German type blossoms into beauty, subtly it disturbs or irritates the Latin. By the same rule, the northern peoples have for centuiies made Frenchmen, Italians, or Spaniards their stage villains. The screen personality of Valentino was so extraordinarily attractive, the tragic expressiveness of Jannings is so overwhelming, as to overcome instinctive prejudices; they, however, are among the exceptions which prove the rule. When Douglas Fairbanks and Mary Pickford went abroad, Madrid, Rome, and Paris welcomed them as hysterically as London, Moscow, and Berlin. Curiously, Lasky adds, the British have the same quality. Though other races may dislike the abstract Empire, they cherish no aversion to the concrete type. However, the Briton's lifelong training in repression of emotion hampers him as a pantomimist. Our manners have run to the other extreme; while we do not weep with the unrestrained naturalness of the Latin, generally we throw our emotions to the surface. Perhaps the British will learn the trick. That is why some of our lords of the moving picture believe that the menace to our supremacy will come—if it ever does come—not from Berlin but from London.

Finally, war or no war, Europe would have encountered eventually the same financial obstacle—the population and the per-capita wealth which enable us, before we send a film abroad, to spend with millionaire lavishness on a production and get our money back from the domestic sales.

Perhaps the "talking movie" is on its way; perhaps within a decade managers may present Hampden in Shakespeare or Gémier in Molière, with complete illusion of motion and voice. How that may effect the "silent drama," no one can guess. Certainly, the talking film cannot become international like the one-dimensional picture of to-day. Hampden's productions will go only to the English-speaking countries, Gémier's only to France and her colonies. If its vogue supplants that of the older form, the international motion-picture business will simply fall apart into national groups. Artistically this would mark an advance, probably; but socially a retro-gression. Whatever may be the sins of the silent film nothing else in history has so advanced that world-wide acquaintance between peoples which is the beginning of understanding. Unconsciously, those fur workers, small salesmen, clothing operatives, and vaudeville performers who brought the moving picture out of the back streets, were creating the first universal language of mankind.

CHAPTER XX

EXIT MARY PICKFORD

*T*HE historian dealing with circumstances as complex as those which gathered round Adolph Zukor in 1916 must take one important thread at a time and follow it to its end; otherwise he is writing only annals and chronology. When I branched off into the adventures of the American film abroad, I left Zukor in control of his own distribution and in the act of paying Mary Pickford $10,000 a week. Her relations with Zukor's firm then and subsequently have their important bearing on the history of the moving picture.

Mary Pickford, said the business, was Adolph Zukor's mascot. When finally he lost her, pessimists and detractors prophesied his early finish. That stroke of luck —finding Pickford—had made him; her departure would leave Famous Players-Lasky a hollow shell. Indeed, any superficial observer might have said the same. Time and again, this ever-expanding business had drawn near to a danger point when the latest Pickford film, selling even beyond anticipation, hauled it over the peak.

In her memoirs, Ellen Terry calls "working friendship" between men and women the cream of human in-

244

tercourse. On the stage woman first achieved her full freedom; and until the last generation, that sturdy relationship was confined to the stage. From the first, Mary Pickford and Adolph Zukor had one of these working friendships. They are just enough alike to understand, just different enough to admire. Not alone to a golden curl, a pair of soft eyes, and the unfair gift of personality does Mary Pickford owe her astonishing success. Underneath, she has the same hard mind as Adolph Zukor, the same steely persistence, the same all-pervading intelligence, and the same financial shrewdness tempered with generosity. Their temperaments "clicked."

"I always liked his ideas," says Mary Pickford.

"She taught me a great deal. I was only an apprentice then; she was an expert workman," says Adolph Zukor.

On the surface, this understanding expressed itself in a father-and-daughter attitude. A survivor of those symposiums in Daniel Frohman's study remembers that Mary Pickford came one night in a dress with very short sleeves. It worried Adolph Zukor all the evening. She might catch cold; and besides it wasn't exactly modest for a girl of her age! Again one night, a year or so later, Mary Pickford dined with Mr. and Mrs. Zukor at a Broadway hotel. As darkness fell and the white lights of Broadway came out full blaze, Zukor asked her mysteriously to leave the table and follow him. He led her to a window on the mezzanine-floor hall, posed her, bade her look up and tell him what she saw. Down the front of the theatre opposite ran her own name in electric lights—the announcement of her promotion from Class B to Class A. She was to be a great star now, advertised and exploited on a parity with Mrs. Fiske and Hackett. "I suppose there were tears in both our eyes," says Mary Pickford.

Personal feelings, however, did not in the least cramp their style when it came to bargaining and trafficking, any more than it would have hampered them in a friendly game of cards. Otherwise they would have esteemed each other less. When Mary Pickford's star began its rise, she was under contract to Adolph Zukor at $20,000 a year. Shortly other firms were paying lesser luminaries more than that. This she told Adolph Zukor. "All right, let's be happy," said he; and he made it $1,000 a week. Again, after *The Good Little Devil* began sweeping the world, he advanced it to $2,000 a week and then in January, 1916, to $4,000. This was an unprecedented salary for the stage—a third again as much, remarked the newspapers, as we were paying our President; for in that age of comparative innocence we still applied the old measuring rod to incomes.

In the summer of 1916, Mary Pickford's contract with Famous Players-Lasky expired. The whole motion-picture business knew that; the greater companies, then at that stage of existence when a corporation struggles for a sure foothold, prepared for a spirited contest in bidding. At that moment Mary Pickford blazed above all other stars like the ascendant Venus over the constellations. The rise of Charlie Chaplin came a little later; yet Chaplin had just signed with the Mutual Company for $10,000 a week and a bonus. Any firm could afford to lose money on her for the prestige she gave its other productions. At this crisis of her affairs, she was working in Hollywood. Between pictures, she came to New York, the financial centre of the business. The hammering, the polite, insinuating approaches, had begun before she left California. She saw Adolph Zukor, told him frankly that she was worth more money.

"I agree with you," he said; but he made no offer.

"Well, before I sign with anyone else, I'll see you again," said Mary Pickford.

Forth she went to a round of blandishment and entertainment and to a first-class impersonation of feminine hesitation and capriciousness. Half a dozen times the ink was wet on the pen with which she was to have signed; and always at the last moment she drew daintily back. First to raise the ante was an agent of the American Tobacco Company, which still felt disposed to trifle with motion pictures. He offered $7,000 a week. Vitagraph raised it again. John R. Freuler of the Mutual Company, which already had Chaplin, capped the stricture. He laid before her a contract which meant virtually a million a year. There the bidding stopped; it had reached the peak. Mary Pickford had taken pains to keep Zukor informed as to the status of negotiations. Now, the soft blue eyes with steel behind them faced across a desk the hazel eyes with unplumbed depths.

"I'm going to give you half of the profits of your films and a voice in selecting them," said Zukor. "And a guarantee of ten thousand dollars a week. And, Mary, that's my limit. Others may offer you more. But it's as much as I can afford."

Mary Pickford did not stop to haggle. When the Chief spoke in that tone, she knew by experience he meant finality. A little discussion of details, and she was signing the contract. Why she did this, in view of a better offer, puzzled the motion-picture business at the time. There is no mystery about it. "I like to work with him," said Mary Pickford to a confidant. "We have the same ideas. We've been down in the world and up in the world together, and I'm sure of him. And ten thousand a week is enough, Lord knows! Besides, he's established. I don't have to worry about getting my money."

Even yet, Mary Pickford did not realize fully what had happened to her. By instinct, she was still child of the road, worrying lest the ghost fail to walk on Saturday night!

While war gathered and burst upon us, while our volunteers swarmed to arms, while our ships rushed full speed ahead into the North Sea blockade, the motion picture continued on its mad, triumphant course.

Scarcely had Mary Pickford begun work in the Hollywood studio under her new contract when the unrestful
business had another upheaval and Adolph Zukor saw
another creeping danger.

Production, distribution, and exhibition are the three
main branches of the industry. Zukor, by his judiciously
bold stroke in 1912, had revolutionized production; and
by his victory over Hodkinson in 1916 had placed distribution in its modern relation to the business as a
whole. Now, he began to look ahead into the future of
exhibition, and to worry. Moving-picture houses,
springing up like mushrooms all over the United States,
were showing a decided tendency to assemble into
"strings." Next the strings were twisting together into
strong ropes which might yet strangle the producers.
Corporations in New England, the Middle West, and
California owned their ten, fifteen, even twenty-five
new, well-equipped city theatres. They bought on the
wholesale plan. Already, they were beating down prices.
The time might come when the more powerful groups
would combine and hold producers at their mercy. It
was the danger which Zukor had foreseen when he
fought for control of Paramount and of his own distribution; one step further removed, but the same.

However, the impetus which started the industry on
its third great movement toward modern form came
not from Adolph Zukor but from an unexpected source
and in an unexpected manner. J. D. Williams, who got

in Australia a wide education as an exhibitor, and T. L. Tally, who owned many theatres in and about Los Angeles, spawned early in 1917 a brilliant idea "Let the exhibitors own production." With this idea in mind, they incorporated the First National Exhibitors' Circuit. Chaplin and Pickford were still the symbols of supremacy. First National proposed to corner them and the other great stars by offering a virtual partnership and guarantees exceeding even the swollen salaries of the moment. Otherwise, between the first rough scenario of a picture and the twenty-five-cent piece of the spectator at the door, there would be only one profit— that of the associated exhibitors.

Williams and Tally toured the country, selling the idea to theatre owners. The "programme system," then just beginning, galled some of the exhibitors; and the idea of producing for themselves fascinated them all. First National, while it still existed only on paper, signed up so many important exhibitors that the banks gave generous backing. Williams and Tally had been hammering at Chaplin; now began a bidding match for his services between them and Mutual, his present employer. An offer of $1,075,000 for eight two-reel pictures, with certain conditions regarding liberty of expression, won him over. Two-reel pictures, notice, Chaplin was still working in that archaic form, still throwing custard pies. Not until he settled down with First National did he begin to appear as sole star in long films and to achieve with the critical and sophisticated his standing as an artist.

Mary Pickford, however, was still the first prize. And again she was straining at the leash. After she signed the $10,000-a-week contract, Famous Players-Lasky sent her to the Hollywood studio. Zukor, "whose ideas she liked," remained in New York, growing more and more absorbed in business, paying less and less attention to art. The lot at Hollywood had grown into a veritable factory, with the eight or ten productions going on at once. The management had of course become complex, a little impersonal. The intimate touch of those old days when they threshed out scenarios in Daniel Frohman's apartment had passed forever. The silver cord of personal understanding frayed and snapped. Aware of this, First National approached her with its blandishments. Presently she was in New York again, receiving homage and attention. "A share of the profits, your own way as an artist, and $250,000 guarantee on each picture," said First National. Mary Pickford carried the news to Zukor; he had heard it already. Hammered by two factions in his company—Pickford and anti-Pickford—he had thought out his answer for himself.

"I'm going to offer you," he said, "just what you're worth to me. That's a share of the profits and $225,000 guarantee a picture."

"This time, I'm not going to sign with you for less

than anyone else offers me," replied Mary Pickford. The meeting was formal; both were drawing a front of cold, commercial efficiency over inner fires of emotion. Mary Pickford went back to the headquarters of First National. And the next day she called up Zukor on the telephone.

"I'm about to sign that contract with First National," she said. "Have you anything to say to me?"

"Only God bless you, Mary, and I wish you well!" said Adolph Zukor. And so after five years, during which she had risen from a minor actress to a world celebrity, Mary Pickford departed from Famous Players.

Zukor, walking it out and thinking it out, had reached one of his far-sighted conclusions. Mary Pickford, for all her value, was reducing him to the position of a tail to the kite. The large corporation which he had built, the larger business combination which he envisaged, could not forever depend upon the uncertainty of one human personality. "Better to let her make her way for awhile, and go on our own," he said at the conferences in his office. Some day, he felt, she would come back; and meantime he would have proved that Famous Players-Lasky was bigger than any one star.

In that last expectation, his foresight failed. He is far-thinking, but not after all a prophet. Within a few months, the kaleidoscope turned again and the business assumed another of its dazzling new patterns. This time perhaps the first definite movement came from a schism in his own office force.

When Paramount so dramatically elected Hiram Abrams president, he assumed the management of the re-oriented company, and remained in that capacity after Famous Players-Lasky took it in as a subsidiary. Zukor promoted Ben Schulberg from the press department, and installed him as assistant manager. From the first, the aggressive Abrams and the dominant Zukor worked badly in harness; by 1918 came friction so severe that it began to burn out the bearings. Zukor took the extreme course: he discharged Abrams. Now Schulberg, as he says himself, is a one-man dog. In old days he had been fiercely loyal to Zukor; serving under Abrams, he transferred his allegiance. He sat half that night in Zukor's house, quarrelling with the Boss.

"If he goes, I go," he said.

"Very well, Ben," replied Zukor, at the end of his persuasiveness, "but you'll come back some day."

The prophecy touched off Schulberg's temper.

"I'll come back when you send for me, not before!" he stormed as he bounced out of the room.

(Eight years later Zukor offered Schulberg, who had adventured much in the meantime, the position of production manager at Hollywood. Schulberg could not restrain himself from saying, "Well, you sent for me!" "Yes," said Zukor. "What's a little pride between friends? You've learned a lot while we've lived apart, and you'll be much more useful to us.")

Burning for eminence and revenge, Schulberg and Abrams sat for days analyzing the motion-picture business in its larger aspects, looking for an opening. "And we found one as wide as the Grand Cañon," said Schulberg. First National intended to do away with all middlemen—one profit from studio to box office. But the stars, even though they enjoyed a share in the profits, must divide earnings with the company. Why should not the great stars, solely and entirely, own the producing company? Abrams and Schulberg made a list of the supremely eminent—Mary Pickford and Charlie Chaplin, of course, the new-risen Douglas Fairbanks, W. S. Hart, David Wark Griffith. All these had elastic agreements with their employers or were nearing the termination of existing contracts. A week of intense thought and calculation, then Abrams and Schulberg started for Hollywood with a complete plan in their portfolios. They had managed for two years the biggest system of distribution in the United States. They proposed to perform that function for the new company, and to take for recompense twenty per cent. of the gross receipts— they of course paying the expenses of distribution. That would yield a handsome profit.

To the day of his death, Hiram Abrams declared that he and Ben Schulberg jointly invented the plan which flowered into United Artists. The stars assembled in this galaxy tell a story somewhat different. When First National began to talk of middlemen's profits, these five great figures of the screen—who one and all owe their eminence not only to art and personality but to shrewd minds—had themselves carried reasoning a step further. Their personalities were the staple of this business, the indispensable element. Why should they pay a producing company its heavy profits? They edged together; discussed, even to details, the possibility of a business owned by its talent. Even before Abrams and Schulberg erupted into Hollywood, United Artists was on its way.

These accounts are not irreconcilable. And at any rate, the complete and well-considered plan of Abrams and Schulberg was the agent which crystallized the solution. Chaplin, first approached, listened and promised to enter the combination "if the others would." Fairbanks, Mary Pickford, and Griffith gave the same tentative answer. Hart, at first favourable, withdrew on second thought. The great vogue of the "Western" was passing; romantic plays in modern and familiar setting were sweeping the boards. He had now smaller box-office value than the other four; he feared lest their superior drawing power would thrust him into a corner. The rest, tutored in business technique by Abrams and Schulberg, proceeded with a tentative organization. The news spread through Hollywood, of course. Lasky relayed it over hot wires to Zukor. Rumour exaggerated United

Artists into a "talent trust" which would eventually absorb all the actors and directors, great and small, and produce not only the super-film of Pickford, Chaplin, and Fairbanks but the staple programme-films of the rank and file.

The rumour of a trust was perturbing; and the situation at best looked bad enough. Griffith, Hart, and Fairbanks all belonged now to Zukor's artistic forces; the rising Fairbanks, indeed, had begun to compensate him for the loss of Mary Pickford. Again Zukor hurried West. Amidst the glittering interior decorations of the new Hollywood there were meetings, conferences, and arguments which broke at times into emotion. Schulberg had drawn up "Eighty-nine Reasons for United Artists," designed to cover every possible point of argument. Fairbanks said afterward, "One night I was up against Zukor. When he had me going and I felt like crying, I would go out into the hall and read over my copy of the Eighty-nine Reasons until I got a grip on myself." But the four stars held firm.

Then, just as they were all ready to sign, a counsellor of one of the stars saw a perturbing danger. Mary Pickford's marriage with Owen Moore was drawing to its inevitable close. Everyone on the inside anticipated the divorce which came a year later.

"Suppose now," said this objector, "Mary Pickford does get a divorce and Zukor orders his publicity department to hammer on that point? Mary stands to the American public for fresh, girlish innocence. A divorce story, rightly handled, could hurt her a lot. And Zukor's a ruthless fighter."

Angry though he was with Zukor, Schulberg kept his sense of justice.

"He's a fighter, all right," he replied, "the toughest that is. But there's one thing he'll never do—bring up a personal issue, especially against Mary Pickford. You can bet your bottom dollar on that. Don't I know him?"

Still, the galaxy hesitated. If Zukor wouldn't do such a thing, some other rival might. Then someone had the idea which resolved the situation. Just after the Armistice, Douglas Fairbanks had formed a pleasant acquaintance with William A. McAdoo, Secretary of the Treasury. The Wilson administration was falling to pieces. McAdoo, Lane, and most of the other Cabinet officials were looking round for positions in private life. The President's son-in-law, the arbiter of American business during the war, already a contender for the Democratic nomination—McAdoo's name would lend impregnable respectability. At a salary of $100,000 a year, he became chief counsel for United Artists. And now, the galaxy signed up; went ahead.

Only, as McAdoo analyzed the new organization he put his finger on a weak spot.

"The stars own their business and take all the profits clear to the box office—that's the idea, isn't it?" he asked. "Very well. Now here, right in the middle, you're giving Abrams and Schulberg twenty per cent. of the gross and letting them make their profit. You ought to own that, too." Abrams and Schulberg saw that his logic was past argument. After some haggling, they accepted an offer of two per cent. of the gross receipts in lieu of salary, United Artists to pay all expenses.

Fairbanks was now gone forever from Famous Players, and Mary Pickford, and Griffith. Yet Zukor, as he rushed east to his office, felt a sense of relief. This was not a trust in formation. It did not intend to gather up all the talent, small and large, under one tent—a process which might lead in the end to general degradation of the business. It was just a company of first-rate stars, presenting a "high-class product." On those terms he could compete. As cheerful as ever, he glided into the anxious conferences awaiting him in his offices; began at once to lay out a new programme for the next year.

He threw to the fore screen versions of best-selling novels and dramas with long Broadway runs. He retained still such tried and successful actors as Pauline Frederick and Blanche Sweet. Gloria Swanson, rising fast, presently stood peer to Mary Pickford; Tommy Meighan filled the hole which Fairbanks had left. Famous Players-Lasky expanded as usual, returned dividends as usual. In 1916, the trade papers, with inner apologies to the gods of truth, had echoed the press agent who called it a $25,000,000 combination. In 1919, the sober financial statement at the annual meeting showed that it was a $37,000,000 combination. Zukor had grown, but so had the whole business. No longer, perhaps, did he run at the head of the pack. But at least he was in the thin front line of the van. And then, as now, he stood symbol for leadership in his business, like Ford in automobiles or Gary in steel.

CHAPTER XXI

THE SOIL OF THE EARTH

WE HAVE reached 1919, the year of the peace. Seven
years now since Adolph Zukor took the fate of an industry into his own hands and plunged; and in the complicated story of his acts during this period I have somewhat neglected the man. As his fortunes expanded, so
did his scale of living. First it was the apartment in
Eighty-eighth Street, then a mansion on Riverside
Drive. The urge for exercise and the habit of keeping
fit persisted. But he had "slowed up" for tennis, as do
most men in their forties. With equal enthusiasm he
took to golf, and entered the innumerable company of
those who "play around a hundred." He found time
now and then for a little bridge or poker—at which he
is as proficient as one might expect—and to indulge at
opera or symphony his passion for music. A sociable
being, he entertained lavishly. Otherwise he worked
and thought.

All this time there were worrisome, perplexing private
troubles. The surviving Zukors and their wide connection by marriage were feeling the tragedy of all international families in the late war. It lacked only the
supreme tragedy: divided allegiance. So far as the

American branch retained any interest in European politics, they held the old-fashioned Hungarian attitude toward the Dual Monarchy and the German alliance. The Dual Monarchy was a convenience, a temporary arrangement binding them to no loyalty of sentiment toward Germans either of the north or of Austria. But the blow had fallen; willing or unwilling, their European kinsmen must go into the ranks. The thing was stripped to its human values—pure calamity. Before the war ended, thirty-eight men of the Zukor-Kohn-Kaufmann connection abroad wore uniforms; and after we entered, eight of the American branch. Young Eugene Zukor, far below draft age, enlisted in the Navy. Al Kaufmann became a captain in the Signal Corps, fought overseas, then remained abroad to manage Paramount's European theatres. Matching notes after the war, one of the American clan found that he had lain for a week in the trenches firing at an Austrian company in whose ranks served his own cousin!

During the first two years, the American clan, and Zukor especially, helped support the women and children among their European kinsfolk. They, like all women and children of Europe, were struggling along with farm and shop while the breadwinner fought at the front. Owing to his temperament, Rabbi Arthur Liebermann was a special problem. His brother sent remittances for his support and comfort. They lasted just one day. The Rabbi would collect the money, take it to the railroad station where the refugees were pouring in before the Russian attacks on the eastern frontier, and give it all away. Zukor was arranging to guard Rabbi Liebermann against his own generosity when the red cloud settled upon us also, and remittances must cease— for sending money to a relative on the other side of the barrier constituted technical disloyalty.

Throughout the war, Zukor and all the family connection were shipping their concentrated product in increasing quantities and at increasing prices to all the Allied nations. Yet by odd circumstance, the Allies practically excluded their persons. American citizens all, they were nevertheless "of enemy birth or origin." Even though they forced or cajoled an entrance into Great Britain, France, or Italy, they would live and move under espionage and dark suspicion. When in 1916 Charlie Chaplin signed his contract for $10,000 a week, the British press stormed and fulminated at this born Briton who remained in America making money while the Empire stood in peril. Only a manœuvre of commercial propaganda, this. With exactly the same motive and inspiration, the British press denounced *The Big Parade* in 1925 as "a piece of Yankee boastfulness"— while from the Hebrides to the Lizard it packed houses and scored record runs.

It needed but one unforeseen incident to start a hue and cry, just as insincere, against these Americans of "enemy origin" who were cutting so deeply into an

Allied industry. The clan sat quiet in America, carrying on the business. When we entered, they gave their sons to our armies, their treasure to our war-chest. As our government, somewhat tardily, organized its own foreign propaganda, it incorporated the film into the general plan. William A. Brady became temporarily chaperon and dictator of the moving picture in its relations with the war. Just before Germany broke, our official films were ready. Thenceforth until the sudden end, all American programmes going abroad carried twenty-five per cent. of propaganda pictures.

The war drew to its victorious end. Zukor had worked like a truck horse and thought like a dynamo for six years, during which he had led a minor business into the state of a major American industry. Both the war and the necessities of the job had denied him those leisurely jaunts through Europe by which habitually he restores his forces. In all that period, he had taken no real vacation. Again, his nerve ends cried out with fatigue; the itching irritation of his skin was becoming chronic. The specialists advised a long rest. That was impossible to Zukor; but he could change his way of living. With his own large sanity, he decided to drop the life of Manhattan with its exciting dazzle, its cloying allurement.

In a bend behind the palisades of the Hudson he found an estate of three hundred acres with a substantial stone house. Here he established himself. When he made this remove, he was taking it as medicine; the country had never attracted him. But it was as though his background came forward and enveloped him, as though the blood of a thousand ancestors who farmed the hill-slopes of Hungary rose up in his veins. Suddenly, he grew enamoured of the pastoral life. He added seven hundred more acres, transformed the stone building into a kind of communal kitchen, dining room, and living room, connected it by arcades with a guest house and a separate residence for his immediate family. As years went on, bringing a fantastic increase of income, he laid out a private golf links, a gardened swimming pool below gardened tennis courts, greenhouses, herds of blooded stock, even a little theatre for private exhibitions of moving pictures.

From his office on Times Square, his automobile takes him in less than an hour, his power boat in less than forty minutes, to the gates of this estate. And it seems a thousand miles from Broadway. The Palisades, sloping on their landward side to abrupt hills, rim it to eastward as with a segment of a bowl. The houses stand on a series of knolls which look even to the maroon hazes of distance over clipped meadow and thick forest. Through its heart a brook, alive with brown trout, cuts for itself a miniature cañon and drops over a waterfall. The district surrounding Zukor's find dwells an hour from Broadway in a state of pastoral innocence. The pioneers were an offshoot from the original Dutch settlers of

New York; the butcher, the banker, the grocer, the farmers on abutting lands bear Knickerbocker names. But alas, the realtor has of late discovered this charming Sleepy Hollow and wayside boardings are beginning to forecast its doom!

This country home has become Zukor's hobby. Eight months of the year he leads here an existence surrounded by sturdy comfort and unostentatious luxury. When winter banks the roads and locks the Hudson, he either makes one of his dashes to Europe or establishes himself in a hotel suite. For the rest of the year—four days a week he goes to the office by automobile or motor boat and works with all his vicious concentration, but Friday, Saturday, and Sunday he keeps for his own and stays on the farm. A round or two of golf, long walks wherein he inspects and plans, a game of bridge or a pre-view of a new film, much pleasant sociability—that has become his real life.

A visitor found him regarding one of his tall fir trees, just felled for a flag pole. He looked up. "It's a pity to kill a thing so beautiful," he said, "I like to preserve, not kill." Then his eye wandered over the vistas of his broad acres. "There wouldn't be much satisfaction about a place like this," he commented, "if someone else did it all for you. Planning it yourself and seeing it grow— that's the joy. I suppose I'll be improving this farm until I die!"

Here of late he has held his important conferences

with heads of departments; here for week-ends come such lords of finance and politics as have high business with the screen. The guest book is almost a roster of American eminence. Perhaps the atmosphere is most characteristic, however, on those off-weeks when there are no celebrities in the guest house and the clans of Zukor, Kaufmann, and Kohn gather. On his relatives by marriage, Zukor exercises his complex for the blood-relationships of which fate robbed him. Sometimes he sits at the head of the great table in the dining room with forty relatives-in-law strung out before him. There is, too, the nursery, where play the four babies presented to him by those satisfactory children, Eugene and Mildred. A delegation of European moving-picture producers, coming to Zukor for a conference of international importance, found him on the lawn, fifth member to a game of tag. . . . His studios and offices have sensed the growth of this paternal and patriarchal quality; and his office nickname—behind his back—is "Papa Zukor."

Father to Ricse also! When the war ended, when Bela Kuhn's impermanent government fell, when the Treaty of Sèvres tore Hungary from her Austrian alliance on one side and her rich Transylvanian provinces on the other, the triangle of grain-fields and vineyards between Ricse, Szanto, and Szalka knew hard, uncertain distress. An economic system had been torn limb from limb; the wounds bled. Ricse had food, perhaps, but little else.

Even before pathetic after-war letters brought news of past bereavement and present distress, the newspapers had reported the quandary of rural Hungary. Zukor ventured on his first European trip in nearly five years. He proceeded to Budapest. Rail traffic was paralyzed, and, in the disturbed political condition, the dictator had forbidden the country roads to automobile traffic. Zukor employed a lawyer and a man of business, both wounded veterans of the war, chartered a motor hand-car, and ran down to his birthplace. After a conference with the town council, Zukor set up his own relief organization. The lawyer and the man of business sat at a desk; Zukor established himself behind a screen, listening unseen to Ricse as it filed past, telling its troubles. This woman needed a major operation, but she had no money even to get her to Budapest, where there were hospitals and good surgeons. This woman's husband had died in the war, and there were six children to support. This farmer had come home disabled with wounds, and Hungary could grant no funds for relief of its human wreckage. This brood of five children had lost their father in battle, their mother in the distress that followed dismemberment of the Empire. At night, Zukor took the lists of cases and set down opposite each name a sum of money; noted, according to circumstances, whether it should be a loan or a gift. Superficial distress relieved, he went deeper into the economic structure of the district. He financed the important flour mill—of which his uncle Ignatz was still main owner—and the winery; showed them the way to find regular markets. Now, half of Ricse corresponds with Adolph Zukor; one transatlantic mail brings him sometimes forty or fifty letters. He keeps for his Ricse correspondence a special drawer of his desk; sometimes when Eugene Zukor bounces into the office with the announcement that the car is waiting, he finds his father running over the naïve and pathetic epistles, and has to call him back four thousand miles to the Broadway of reality. . . . And when he goes to Budapest nowadays, the lively, attractive Hungarian world of art and letters hails him like a crowned monarch.

CHAPTER XXII

THE CAPSTONE

DAVID WARK GRIFFITH and Adolph Zukor had in the old obscure days worked side by side in Fourteenth Street: the one as a director, throwing his own stories on the screen at a salary of fifty dollars a week; the other as a minor exhibitor, wringing small and precarious profit from five-cent admissions. When the tide of fortune began racing, they rode it together. However, their careers, while running parallel, touched only once. In 1917, after many fruitless efforts, Zukor tempted Griffith with a salary of $3,000 a month and drew him into the producing staff of Famous Players. Now, less than two years later, Griffith had left him to enter United Artists. Zukor, having failed to prevent this formidable combination, was departing from Hollywood when Griffith met him. And they talked over the situation with the brutal frankness of old friends.

"I know what you've always wanted to do, Adolph," said Griffith—"lead the world as a super-producer. And for six or seven years you have led. But now the artists have taken things into their own hands. It's our day"— Griffith is to be pardoned if in the fresh enthusiasm of a new venture he overstated the case—"and you must look elsewhere for your supremacy. Meantime, life has forced you to become a man of finance, not an artist. Life's always playing these tricks on us. It's time you began to own theatres. Production is a bit of a gamble. But theatres are bricks and mortar and land. Savage, Ringling, and all the others who have accumulated fortunes from the show business made their big money out of real estate. Loew's doing just that thing right now." So spoke Griffith, he of the uncanny instincts.

The far-sighted Zukor needed no such advice. Three years before, he had begun to see that theatre owners might in the end dictate to producers and distributors. After all, they held the box office; the dam-gate to the flood of gold. But in less than seven years he had revolutionized production in a business which was increasing from millions to billions, had put system into distribution, and had done it on less original capital than it takes to produce one first-class modern feature film. He had neither time, energy, nor capital to spare for this final struggle. Already, the multiplying costs of the business, its rapid expansion, had forced him to go to the public with a modest issue of stock. Moreover, United Artists was a serious threat; to meet it took for a time all his energies. Then came the brief hard times of 1920, when moving pictures suffered along with all other luxuries.

However, one Monday morning Zukor entered the

office in his working mood and telephoned to Felix
Kahn, owner of the Rivoli and Rialto theatres in the
Times Square district. Fifteen minutes, and Kahn was
in his office. Twenty minutes, and Kahn departed. Then
Zukor glided into Lasky's office. The artistic director of
Famous Players was editing a troublesome scenario.

"I've just bought the Rialto and Rivoli theatres as
key houses for first New York showings," said Zukor.
"We've been needing something of the kind for a long
time."

"That's nice," replied Lasky absently, and bent himself again over the scenario.

From this beginning Famous Players-Lasky, acting
through a subsidiary, began judicious purchase of
theatres and partnerships in theatres. First it was a
string in New England, then one in the South including
the Howard at Atlanta. Even so, Famous Players-
Lasky remained a minor figure in exhibition. For once
Zukor was following, not leading. When he began large-
scale production, when he systematized distribution, he
was tilling virgin soil. But a half-dozen producing companies, including the pioneer First National, the eminent United Artists, the sensationally expanding Metro-
Goldwyn, had preceded him into this field. Zukor held
his own through special if impermanent arrangement
with this and that string of independent houses, while
he waited for an opening. It came presently; and again
from the West. This introduces another set of those

immigrant annals which are to our democracy a modest triumph and to Europe a fairy tale.

In 1906 Sam Katz, being then fourteen years old, began to work his way through a Chicago high school. When Sam was less than a year old, his father had fled from oppression in a Russian ghetto, reached Chicago, and, taking the first job that offered, became a barber. In the course of years he acquired a shop of his own. "Like any Russian Jew, he had two ambitions for his son," says Sam Katz, "a general education and an accomplishment." Sam showed a talent for music; so when he was eight years old, his father bought him his first piano lessons at twenty-five cents an hour. However, he had no real musical ambition. As he plotted his life, he intended to work his way through high school, Northwestern University, and law school, and set up as an attorney.

One Saturday night in 1906—the very year when Adolph Zukor seriously entered exhibition—Sam Katz went to a moving-picture show on the South Side. Carl Laemmle owned the house as a modest member of his little string; and a patent-medicine performer with a bifurcated beard managed it. Falling into conversation with the doorkeeper, Sam learned that they needed a pianist. The manager, approached, gave him a tryout. He passed triumphantly.

When at Sunday morning breakfast Sam broke the news to his parents, Katz Senior said, "Why don't you

After the fire. Ruins of the Famous Players studio in Twenty-sixth Street, New York. The safe containing all of the company's films can be seen clinging to the wall to the upper right

The Paramount Building. Housing the Paramount Theatre, leader in the Publix chain of theatres, this building towers thirty-nine stories above Times Square, New York

tell me that you've taken a job as a bartender and be done with it?" and Mrs. Katz wailed. However, on his solemn promise to resist the temptation of this low environment, Sam had his way. During his whole freshman year at high school, he "pounded the box" with an open Latin grammar, for study in odd moments, propped up on the music rack.

One night, just by way of making conversation, Sam Katz asked the patent-medicine man how much their store show made. "Between three and four hundred dollars a week—net," he replied. Three or four hundred a week!

Next morning at breakfast Sam imparted the news to his parents. "If I were you, Dad, I'd can the barber shop—tear out the chairs and turn it into a moving-picture show," he added. "There's millions in it." He glanced up in time to see his parents exchanging suppressed smiles.

Then Abe Baliban, tenor, came to the little Laemmle house with a sentimental song-slide. Their mutual interest in music drew him and Sam Katz together. Both saw millions in moving-picture exhibition. Next autumn— Sam being still in high school—these two and Abe's brother Barney opened a show of their own. It was a converted store, with the marks where the shelves had been still decorating the walls. The audience sat on second-hand benches or decrepit kitchen chairs about a very hot stove. Barney Baliban took the tickets, purchased the films, generally managed the enterprise; Sam Katz played the piano and Abe Baliban sang for the song-slides. So, they saved the hire of two employees.

By the end of Sam's sophomore year in high school, Baliban and Katz had made so much money that they were branching out. They added another show, another, and still another. This last—modest enough by modern standards—was perhaps the most pretentious motion-picture theatre of its period. Sam Katz had recruited ushers from his fellow students in high school, and dressed them in flashy uniforms. Out of the high-school orchestra he selected a pianist, a violinist, and a 'cellist to play incidental music; began even the daring inno-vation of rehearsing them with the film. . . . A dynamic boy, this, also, beyond his abilities and energies he had the unfair gift of personality. As that spruce little figure and that ever-smiling face entered a room the atmosphere seemed to brighten. All men of his kind liked him on sight.

When Sam Katz marched across the platform to get his high-school diploma, he was earning $400 a week; and his skeptical father had long since closed the barber shop and gone to managing one of the Baliban and Katz houses. Sam had found his affairs so pressing that he must needs now and then drop out of school for a term. But he was still steering for his major objective: the law. He had his programme laid out; he would take two years at Northwestern and the full course at law school.

By that time, he hoped to have $50,000 in cold cash
with which he could start a law business and start it
right—no clerkship or minor partnership.

The newspapers were moralizing on "the film craze"
and hinting at its impermanence. Sam Katz more than
half agreed with them. He felt utter contempt for the
trash he was feeding to his public; and certain film
producers whom he had met showed minds and imaginations so limited as to intensify his skepticism. He was
simply working a little bonanza while the boom lasted.
He entered Northwestern, devoting his days to improving and cultivating his mind and his nights to planning
and devising for the Baliban and Katz theatres.

Then in the summer of 1912 a states' rights buyer
offered them that epoch-making film *Queen Elizabeth*.
Baliban and Katz had it projected; and Katz came
away in a blaze of illumination. Here was a four-reel
film, superbly photographed by an artist with the
camera, acted by the greatest figure on the modern
stage. Someone "was putting brains onto the film."
He had been thinking of exhibition on the old terms—
as something akin to saloon keeping and in his special
case a fortunate avenue to a respectable career. For the
first time, he entertained the idea that there was a stable
future in this business. Behind *Queen Elizabeth* came
The Prisoner of Zenda and Mary Pickford's early productions in the long film. These banished all doubt.
The thin vein was opening toward a mother-lode.

The Baliban brothers saw the light also. Within the year—Sam Katz being still a student at Northwestern—they drew up plans and found loans for a great moving-picture palace which they called the Grand Central. Sam Katz was too young to vote, and the Baliban brothers still in their twenties. In their inexperience with big business, they made the usual mistakes. Also, the outbreak of the European war increased the prices of labour and material beyond their calculations. Only the steadily increasing revenues of their small theatres pulled them through.

But early in 1917, the Grand Central, as ambitious a playhouse as the moving picture knew up to that time, opened the doors of its majestic and glittering auditorium. It was legitimate ancestor to such palaces of the moving picture as Roxy's on Seventh Avenue; the same great auditorium, the same gaudy effects of gold and high colour, the same orchestras, scenic effects, vaudeville support. By now, Sam Katz had transferred his ambition, for it seemed foolish to renounce such opportunities. Also, he wanted to get married. In 1916, being then in his twenty-fourth year of age and his second of law school, he closed his books and entered the harbour of matrimony.

Adolph Zukor came out to Chicago for the opening of the Grand Central. Ever since he saw the first Famous Players films, Sam Katz had admired this pioneer. Their

ideas gibed—"a high-class production and nothing else."
In those days, the serial mystery film was sweeping
Chicago. Sam Katz had done his best to keep such
fustian out of his theatres. With approval he noted that
Zukor had never adopted this easy way of making
money. They fell together at once. Zukor had one of his
rare loquacious moments. He talked so eloquently on
the future of films—always provided the producers kept
to a high level—that he left the brilliant boy of twenty-
five his follower and disciple. During the next three
years Baliban and Katz, on the profits of the Grand
Central, opened three more first-class theatres in Chicago
and began to stretch a web of houses through the Middle
West. And they all served unofficially as exhibition out-
lets for Famous Players-Lasky.

In 1920, Zukor and Katz had another long talk, this
one less satisfactory. Production, Zukor remarked incidentally, was the heart of the business; and on this he
disserted at some length. Now Sam Katz was still in his
twenties, and a born enthusiast. To him, the world revolved about exhibition; the producers and distributors
were only feeders to the theatre owner. First National,
owned and conducted by exhibitors, had long been
hammering at Baliban and Katz. Returned to his office,
Sam Katz drew up in parallel columns reasons why and
why not he should throw in the fortunes of the company
with First National. "Some of the reasons, I know now,

were unsound," he says, "but at the moment the 'yeas' appeared to have it."

He won over the Baliban brothers—and entered First National. A year or two more, and he found himself discontented with that connection, veering again toward Zukor. By 1923, Baliban and Katz, through an interlock too complicated for description here, became main outlet for the Famous Players-Lasky films—the connection for which Zukor had been looking. And in 1925 was formed Publix Theatres, a subsidiary of Famous Players-Lasky. It drew in all the Paramount houses in the South and New England, the Baliban and Katz interests, a few smaller strings. Sam Katz, being then but thirty-three years old, came on to New York to serve as manager. Seven Baliban brothers had reached years of discretion; and all work in the Middle West as sub-managers for Publix. There are some seven hundred theatres in this string, including one important house in each "key city"—the towns which set fashions for their subsidiary regions, as Denver for the Rocky Mountains, Atlanta for the Southeast.

At about the same period, Paramount began spotting Europe with big theatres of its own; the "key-city" plan again. Now, the chain runs from Vienna to San Francisco. And as it lengthened, Adolph Zukor, a showman to his bones, conceived the idea of one great, dominant mother-house, symbolical of all his business. Four or five years before he broached this plan to his associates, he bought the property at the northwest corner of Forty-third Street and Broadway; a Southern gate to Times Square. He carried the existing building as a taxpayer until the Publix string was completed; then, in 1926–27, rose the thirty-story Paramount Building; theatre de luxe below, housing for his enterprises above. Roxy's palace of the cinema in Fiftieth Street is probably the last word in glittering, pretentious, tinselled framework for moving pictures. But the Paramount, set cunningly near those entrances of the subway by which most spectators enter the City of Delights, seems to dominate Times Square. Amorphic in some aspects, merely pretentious in others, in still others massive and imposing, its veiled illumination makes it by night all wonder and mystery. And in these contradictions it symbolizes the institution which gave it being—the motion picture with its shallowness and yet its profound influence on international comities, its shimmering beauties and yet its tawdriness, its educative value and yet its defiance of orderly thinking, its realism of scene and setting and yet its romanticism of action and plot. . . .

It stands a symbol in another way—the capstone of a career. Adolph Zukor had now rounded this strange business of his into final form. At all stages, from the raw film to the screen, he controlled his product. Stretching from the Paramount Building round the world ran an organization as delicate as a watch and as regular. Sidney Kent, risen in this last stage to general management under Zukor, is dynamo to its armies of high-priced specialists and experts, its conventions and its pep-clubs. And all about, the motion-picture business has assumed somewhat the same form. The day of the small independent producer has passed. The industry, after all its kaleidoscopic shiftings, has settled down into seven or eight corporations or groups, all of which manage their own distribution and possess or control their own theatres.

New and odd as is this industry of making life out of shadows, it has not escaped the general law of any great American business. Some pioneer starts it on the traditional shoestring. It grows, combines, takes in abutting interests; this brings the need of extensive capital; and it goes to Wall Street. When Zukor began buying theatres, the first modest issue of common stock was followed by a larger double issue of common and preferred; and from then on a bankers' committee sat with the management. The rival firms, generally speaking, have come to the same harbour. And a detached observer seems to behold the first sign of a new struggle, between artists who by instinct waste with the prodigality of nature, and bankers who conserve.

Meantime Famous Players–Lasky, which began in 1912 with Adolph Zukor's little fortune of three or four hundred thousand dollars, reported in 1926 resources of $149,000,000. American business, with its spectacular achievement, has often accomplished such miracles of rapid accumulation. However, in most other cases the astronomical sum of its final capitalization represents values already in existence when the founder began his work. This does not. It is a feat of sheer creation.

CHAPTER XXIII

THE MAN AND THE MIND

As I write, Adolph Zukor is fifty-four years old; and the work is done that he was born to do. Looking out from his tower on late winter afternoons, he beholds a field of glittering electric signs which proclaim the triumph of his idea. They mark the moving-picture houses which, stably and exclusively, hold Times Square. As though in revenge for the days when Broadway snubbed the hoydenish cousin of Union Square, they have pushed the spoken theatre into the side streets. His creation stands rounded and complete. What with his native constitution, his moderation in eating and drinking and his systematic exercise, he may have twenty years of work still in him. But the rest will be an easy pull up a gentle slope. Struggle is over for him—and perhaps his creation.

So, as though he were already dead, we may make some inquiry into the kind of man who wrought these things, and try to answer that eternal question of the success-bound American: "By what qualities denied to me has he risen?"

A question not easy to answer. The real Adolph Zukor lives deep, hidden by reserves and by an instinctive shyness. His very oldest associates, to whom he has clung for the twenty years of his rise, say that although he has expressed his feeling for them by a hundred generosities, they read his affection only in his acts; never has he so much as hinted it by words. Around no man eminent in American business have there gathered so few anecdotes. He does nothing to create anecdote, either by pleasant folly or by flash of wit.

Not that he has a cold personality, even to the casual acquaintance. At all stages of his career men have liked him on sight. He has, to begin with, a masculine comeliness which probably influences subconsciously even his own sex. And his stillness strikes the beholder not as an absence of motion but as a balance between infinite energies—"like a spinning top." He smiles habitually; and when he meets a new acquaintance, he has the air of waiting for him to say something pleasant; of expecting it. Then, as the stranger begins to do business with him, impression of that comely, quietly engaging personality begins to fade; wiped out by perception of that round, full skull, that close mouth with the tight grip over the short, close-biting teeth of a fighter, that radiation of power. . . .

The teeth do not belie his character. He is a fighter, resembling in that one of those soft-stepping, soft-spoken shooting men rated as the most dangerous variety in the old West. Not that he is contentious or quarrelsome. He joins battle only when some human obstacle bars his way to one of his large purposes. Then he fights with everything he has; inside of the rules, but otherwise ruthlessly. He gives no quarter while the struggle is on, though he is perfectly capable, on the day after the armistice, of handing a beaten adversary a stake to start him anew in life. It is impersonal fighting; win or lose, he holds no grudges against a fair adversary. There are those among his intimates who call this his supreme personal quality. "Courage is his secret," says one of them. "Or perhaps I'd better call it pluck. He's a great gambler with life; and long after everyone else has been frightened out of the game, he stays on."

He is crafty in battle, as the story of his struggle with Hodkinson shows, and also supremely resourceful. Once, in the days when the business was shifting like a kaleidoscope, an executive in the firm of Shubert bought a substantial share in a rival motion-picture company. This was that day of triumph for the Shuberts when they had just downed Klaw and Erlanger and seized the supremacy in theatrical booking. It seemed that they were about to enter motion pictures; with their control over houses, they would make most formidable rivals. Broadway scented a new battle. In the capacity of peace maker and friend of both parties, William A. Brady visited Zukor, and proposed a meeting.

"All right, Billy," said Zukor, "but I never go into a fight without a gun."

The newspapers, next morning, explained this cryptic.

Zukor had purchased outright Charles Frohman Inc., a firm left orphaned by Frohman's death on the *Lusitania*. At the moment, it stood unsurpassed for prestige. This was a notice of a counter-invasion. With some difficulty, Brady got Zukor and Lee Shubert, next evening, into a private dining room of Claridge's. They talked nearly all night. None but they knows exactly what happened; but though Shubert kept his motion-picture stock and Zukor owns Charles Frohman Inc. to this day, invasion and counter-invasion stopped there.

Temperamentally, he is a creator, an artist—perhaps in the last analysis those two words are synonyms. He shows that in his very habits of work. Like an artist, he gives himself forth in bursts; periods when what he is doing absorbs all his waking hours, varied with periods of indolent relaxation. In American business, these creative spirits always plough and seldom reap. They set afoot new movements or methods, but usually their temperament unfits them for that second stage, when siege and fruition demand stable organization. Zukor made the transition painlessly; showed himself equally able as an originator and an administrator. His abilities, indeed, seem marvellously fluid. I have told how he astonished Brady with his self-taught expertness at accounting. And no one associated with him in production of moving pictures doubts that, had not circumstances intervened, he might have fulfilled his ambition to become a high artistic director of motion pictures—a figure like Reinhardt on the speaking stage. Two natures work within him: an artist and a man of affairs. But instead of struggling, they have struck a balance.

At balance also stand two seemingly irreconcilable traits: humility and confidence. For all his ambition, he seems little interested in Adolph Zukor. No man I have ever known talked with less ease and relish about himself. I have told how he viewed Jesse Lasky's early pictures and, finding them better than his own, decided to form a combination. He always approaches a rival, they say, in that same spirit—tries to find his points of superiority and learn where he himself is inferior. "A man should love his work," he said in one of his epigrammatic moments, "but when he falls in love with his own work, he's finished!" For all the burning ambition to wield power and to lead which drove him through his thirteen most active years, honours and flatteries mean little to him. . . .

When the Paramount Theatre opened, all Who's Who in New York attended the preliminary reception. Next day, he and Lasky went for a walk and an intimate talk. Passing a Childs Restaurant when Zukor found himself suddenly hungry, they entered and ordered. Suddenly Jesse Lasky laughed. "I was just thinking," he said, "of that splendid ovation yesterday—and here to-day we're lunching at a Childs Restaurant!"

Zukor looked up in surprise. "Why not?" he asked. "The food's good, isn't it?"

Yet when his mind is made up to any course, even the most daring, he proceeds with an utter, calm confidence, which belies this instinctive humility. In 1921, just when he was straining every resource to acquire theatres, broke the famous "Hollywood scandals." The moving-picture stars, attractive young persons suddenly risen from poverty, found themselves possessed of incomes running between $100,000 and $500,000 a year. While most of them spent tawdrily and ostentatiously, they were generally far too busy for much dissipation. Moving-picture acting, under modern conditions, is hard work. A minority, however, behaved as did a minority of the Osage Indians when a quirk of fate threw $12,000 a year into the laps of every man, woman, and child among them. Heavily advertised in their merits, they were advertised also in their defects. Wallace Reid went to pieces, died, was buried to the requiem of newspaper moralists. W. D. Taylor, director, was murdered. No one knows to this day who did it, but gossip radiated from the little, intimate circle of Hollywood to the farthest corner of the globe. Finally came that squalid episode—the death of Virginia Rappe, in Roscoe Arbuckle's hotel apartment. This accidental episode was worse, much worse, for the reputation of the moving picture than any tragedy of intention; the story, as the newspapers began to bring it out, had a soiled and nauseating cast. At the moment "Fatty" Arbuckle figured importantly in the general scheme of Famous

Players-Lasky. They had films of his, mostly unreleased, representing more than a million dollars in cost of production, much more in potential profits.

Zukor did not hesitate even for a day. "Withdraw them," he ordered.

"Permanently?" asked his office force.

"Yes; kill them," said Zukor

And they were withdrawn, though the transaction destroyed most of the year's earnings. Zukor, looking as usual into the future, had formed a plan to meet such an emergency if ever it rose. He approached the executives of the other great companies; within a month, Will H. Hays, politician and church warden, had left the President's Cabinet and sat enthroned as moral dictator of the American moving picture—Cato of a voluntary censorship.

A successful administrator, Zukor has, of course, his skill in picking men, his art in managing them. He likes long-term service. He will reach out and grab a star actor as quickly as any manager; for what a star can do he has already learned from that screen which is the only test. He is slower in selecting an executive; he keeps his prospect under observation for some time—as he did, for example, in the case of Sam Katz. For "what a man does to-day he will do next Monday," he says. Once employed, Zukor likes to keep him for life. In managing men, he conceals the iron hand under the velvet glove. Now and then, in face of utter stupidity or treachery,

his old temper breaks forth. The intelligent and efficient
he manages in such way as not to let them know that
they are being managed.

"I have worked with him for fifteen years," says one
of his veterans, "and I've made my serious mistakes.
Never yet has Zukor reproved me. Only when the crisis
is over, and I realize as well as anyone what I've done,
he glides into my office and says, 'Next time do it this
way. . . .'"

These, however, are only external characteristics.
Let us get at the mind underneath.

The contradictory mixture of humility with confidence and over-veering ambition derives probably from
some knot of consciousness tied in the early, obscure
vears of childhood—an inferiority complex compounded
of his obscure, unhappy origins, his smallness of stature,
his shadowing by a brilliant brother whose powers
blossomed earlier. Such an implanted trait, developing
its abnormal protective mechanism, runs in some able
spirits into arrogance; as witness the comparatively
mediocre Mussolini and the genius Napoleon. Zukor has
avoided this defect of his qualities, and the cause,
probably, lies partly in his steely will and partly in the
character of his intelligence.

Governing his impulses and emotions sits enthroned
the diamond-hard mind of his race. It is a realistic intelligence. Almost passionately, it tries to see things as
they are, whether those things concern Adolph Zukor

or some hated rival or merely an abstract problem.

There are two classes of high intelligence. The possessor of one kind is called by the shallow a creature of instinct. He seems to leap to conclusions of absolute soundness. In reality, he has not leaped, but only run. His mind has passed so swiftly from premise to deduction that he cannot remember the steps; is, indeed, generally unconscious of them.

The other type, while it does not exactly plod, goes more slowly. Before it takes the next step, it establishes itself firmly on every rung of the ladder. It is fully conscious of each stage in its journey. In case of error, it can go back and find the point where it departed from logical sequence. For all the brilliant miracles of the leaping mind, this walking mind is probably the more useful to men of affairs. Among world figures, Arthur Balfour, Woodrow Wilson, and Herbert Hoover belong to this mental caste. These are, or were, all men of finished education; working, too, in the broadest field of activity known to man. Their minds have therefore a wider scope than that of Adolph Zukor; but possibly no more power and skill in resolving a complex immediate problem.

Many have noted this about him: he sits during most of the first hour of a conference or negotiation—to the perception of an uninformed stranger the least noticeable figure about the table. Then he begins to talk, and he dominates the next hour. As the others gave their data and views, he has been reducing them to their essential terms, building up step by step his own course of action until he comes to one of those sound determinations from which he seldom swerves.

He is one half of a good reporter. He goes through the world with his eyes open, an acute collector of facts, human sidelights, even gossip. Remember that when he decided seriously to enter moving-picture exhibition, he studied the business in every aspect. But this acquisitive accumulation does not come forth in oral or written expression. Except in rare moments of relaxation, he avoids reminiscence. By a habit which has grown on him he states any old transaction of his complex career in its simplest, lowest terms. That vital struggle for control between production and distribution, for example—ask him about it, and he will answer, probably something like this:

"Then I saw that we had to have a system of distribution; and so we formed Paramount. After a year or so, I saw that the distributors were going to strangle distribution if they kept on. So I got control of Paramount." Nothing more. His mind is a crucible into which he loads the raw ore of observation and draws it out pure steel; and then he wields that steel in action.

Not that he is inarticulate. Able men, when they care to express themselves, never are. However, Zukor talks most easily and naturally on abstractions and general principles—of his business, of politics, of life. In such discussion, he looses eloquence, an epigrammatic faculty almost poetic at times and even a sly, perceptive humour. I was present when a visitor maintained in friendly argument that sex is the foundation-stone of the moving picture.

"It is?" inquired Zukor. "Did *The Birth of a Nation* depend on sex? Did *The Covered Wagon* or *The Big Parade* or *The Ten Commandments* ? Or any other of the films which we managers advertise as epoch-making? The story's the foundation of the whole structure. If it's a good story that depends on sex, well and good. If it's a good story that doesn't depend on sex, just as good. Everyone of course likes a pretty, attractive woman. It's part, and a very pleasant part of the scheme of life which we're trying in our imperfect way to put onto the screen. Those directors who make their films drip with sex confess their own shallowness and inexpertness. They're unable to tell a really first-class story, so they try to save themselves by sensationalism. It's like the political orator who hasn't anything more to say and knows he's stuck, and so he goes on: 'Behold the starry banner, the proud symbol of our freedom.'"

A turbulent, sparkling river, with rapids, lapping of waves on the shore, whirling eddies. It seems to the eye that these manifestations of power contain the power itself. They do not. Underneath, unseen motive-power of these striking manifestations, runs the current—

puissant, quiet, undisturbed. So on the surface of the
business which Adolph Zukor founded move and flash
blazing display, shallow, glittering advertising, tinsel
decoration. But underneath, motive-power of all, has
run for fifteen years the deep, placid consciousness of
this man.

THE END